# SCHOOL CHOICE
## AND
# DIVERSITY

**What the Evidence Says**

# SCHOOL CHOICE AND DIVERSITY

## What the Evidence Says

---

**JANELLE T. SCOTT**

Editor

---

*Foreword by Henry M. Levin*

**TEACHERS COLLEGE PRESS**

Teachers College, Columbia University
New York and London

Table 8.1 and its discussion first appeared in "Achieving Equality of Educational Opportunity in the Wake of Judicial Retreat from Race Sensitive Remedies: Lessons from North Carolina" originally published in the *American Law Review, 52*(6). Used by permission.

Table 8.2 and its discussion is derived from "The Academic Consequences of Desegregation and Segregation: Evidence from the Charlotte-Mecklenburg Schools" originally published in the *North Carolina Law Review, 81*(4). 81 N.C.L. Rev. 1513 (2003). Used by permission.

Published by Teachers College Press, 1234 Amsterdam Avenue, New York, NY 10027

*Library of Congress Cataloging-in-Publication Data*

School choice and diversity : what the evidence says / Janelle T.
    Scott, editor ; foreword by Henry M. Levin.
        p.   cm.
    "Papers presented at a conference sponsored by the National
Center for the Study of Privatization in Education (NCSPE) at
Teachers College, Columbia University"—Foreword.
    Includes bibliographical references and index.
    ISBN 0-8077-4599-5 (cloth : alk. paper)
        1. School choice—United States—Congresses.   2. Segregation
in education—United States—Congresses.   I. Scott, Janelle T.
LB1027.9.S28      2005
379.1'11'0973—dc22                                     2005043958

ISBN 0–8077-4599-5 (cloth)

Printed on acid-free paper
Manufactured in the United States of America

12   11   10   09   08   07   06   05       8   7   6   5   4   3   2   1

# Contents

# Foreword

In the main, American families choose where their children will attend school. Most families search for a residential location with access to good public schools. Some choose a private school. A smaller number select from among public schools within urban areas, choosing, for example, magnet schools or charter schools. But poor and minority families in inner cities and rural areas do not have such choices, despite their desire for a good education for their children. Such families are too poor to choose the better neighborhoods that harbor good schools, and housing discrimination is a further barrier to access. Even when public school choices are available in urban areas, they are often limited in student openings, and travel distances are prohibitive in rural areas.

Thus, advocates of poor and minority populations have argued increasingly for publicly funded educational vouchers that would enable their children to seek private schooling alternatives. Although the main claim for such a plan is to enlist competition in the marketplace to raise school quality and provide alternatives to those that lack them, a different set of questions can also be raised. Will such choice plans for inner-city children increase racial and income diversity of schools, reflecting a more democratic ideal, or further reduce such diversity?

Although public school desegregation efforts have met with some success in some locations, it appears that most urban areas of the United States are more segregated today than they were in the past. Will educational choice through vouchers and other forms of marketplace privatization be the solution to better education and greater racial and income diversity?

Detractors have argued the opposite by pointing out that White flight from cities and other forms of choice have been the predominant causes of school segregation. They believe that in the long run, the political dynamics pushing for educational vouchers would extend this option to all families. And they further argue that the extent of White and middle-income exodus from schools with diverse populations would overwhelm any improvements in diversity resulting from the escape from inner-city schools. At issue is whether school choice—and especially educational vouchers—would increase ethnic, racial, and income diversity of schools or reduce it.

For this purpose the National Center for the Study of Privatization in Education (NCSPE) at Teachers College, Columbia University convened a conference of scholars who had studied choice processes and their consequences for student diversity. Their contributions were thoughtful and provocative. Janelle Scott, who was assistant director of the NCSPE (and is now a faculty member at New York University) undertook the orchestration of the conference and the editing of the papers for publication. In addition, she invited other authors with pertinent perspectives to contribute their work to this volume.

The result is an immensely valuable work that captures the many dimensions of the issues and controversies as well as buttressing them with data. If there is one conclusion that seems to be universally supported in this complex landscape, it is that context matters greatly in terms of what is likely to happen to student diversity under different choice approaches. The NCSPE owes a debt of gratitude to Professor Scott for bringing this important work together in published form. We also wish to thank the Ford Foundation and the Pew Trusts for providing the funding for the conference and this publication.

Henry M. Levin

# SCHOOL CHOICE
## AND
# DIVERSITY

## What the Evidence Says

# Introduction

## The Context of School Choice and Student Diversity

### JANELLE T. SCOTT

In this book, we examine the empirical research on school choice and student diversity so as to inform the policy debates on their relationship. In so doing, we hope to widen the conversation on school choice beyond policy rhetoric or advocacy-based research, thereby attending to the complexities raised by the expansion of myriad school choice options in a political context of educational inequity and high-stakes accountability. We take for granted that meaningful school choices as well as diversity are valuable social goods—though their relative value is contested—and that there are multiple meanings in the concepts of "choice" and "diversity."

Among the social values that Americans embrace, two are held especially dear: social cohesion and freedom of choice (Levin, 2000). That is, the public holds in high esteem the ideal of a diverse and pluralistic society in which the government has minimal involvement in the lives of its citizens (Levin, 2000; Marshall, Mitchell, & Wirt, 1989). As with many political values, choice and diversity are often in conflict. Perhaps nowhere is this conflict more pronounced than around the issue of school choice, where positions in support of and against choice can be deeply entrenched.

Despite ideological stances that define choice in specific, and often narrow, policies, *school choice* is actually an umbrella term referring to a range of policy options that have had unique histories and have served multiple purposes. In recent years, school choice options have grown to include tuition tax credits, charter schools, vouchers, magnet schools, inter- and intradistrict choice plans, alternative schools, home schooling, online and "virtual" schools, and the private management of public schools. Choice programs are not just distinct from one plan to another; within any given choice reform are differences in design and implementation. Thus, while some school choice plans have the potential to diversify schools, others can further segregate students within and across schools.

For example, without safeguards—such as the provision of equal access to transportation, information, and admissions—the expansion of school choice often coincides with the increased segregation of students and schools by race, social class, gender, ability, and language (Fuller, Elmore, & Orfield, 1996; Metcalf, 2001; Wells, Holme, Lopez, & Cooper, 2000). Parents with better access to information, resources, and social networks have more power to secure the schools of their choosing than do parents with lesser access. In the meantime, many schools engage in formal and informal choice processes when shaping their student populations, and high-poverty families are often the least desirable (Wells, 2002). As a result, choice schools have admissions and expulsion policies that could result in relatively more privileged, and less diverse, student populations.

Still, largely because of the moral triumphs of civil rights era advocates and the value placed on American pluralism, the public tends to look unfavorably upon educational policies that intentionally segregate students (Ball, 2001). Yet regulatory remedies, such as busing or the revision of attendance boundaries, are often unpopular, since Americans look askance at policies that limit choices—these remedies are derisively referred to as "forced choice." With the expansion of school choice reforms, we must decide how to create policies that can negotiate the inherent tensions between choice and diversity (Stone, 2002).

## COMPLEXITY AND CONTEXT

As school choice options continue to grow, so too does the need to examine their effects on student diversity. Parents, teachers, and students interact with public and private school choices in increasingly complex social, economic, educational, and political contexts. These contextual complexities, however, are belied by simplistic claims made by staunch advocates and opponents alike, which tend to be "heavy on theory and light on empirical evidence" (Fowler, 2003).

For example, market-based adherents regard school choice as something of a "battering ram" that will break down the "government monopoly" over schooling, while defenders of traditional public education forms liken school choice to a "Trojan horse," surreptitiously bent on destroying public schools. Yet because the ideal of diversity and equity hold moral currency, many choice advocates and detractors will emphasize the positive and negative effects choice has on diversity, even if diversity is far from the primary concern.

The attendant research framed by these advocacy-based positions produces confusion on the part of the public and further debate between researchers and policymakers (Fowler, 2003; Winerip, 2003). More nuanced research, which tends to reveal the importance of context, gets lost or ignored amid these rancorous debates (Dwyer, 2002; B. Fuller, 2000; Heubert, 1997; Miron & Nelson, 2002; Pleasants, 2000). Choosers are left to sort through confusing claims as they try to make informed selections in an arena of ever expanding educational choices that have disparate origins and serve different political and educational purposes.

## THE EXPANSION OF SCHOOL CHOICES: WHY CONTEXT MATTERS

While some choice options were developed intentionally to address student diversity, others have no stake in the issue. Still, observers have noted that some forms of choice can exacerbate or increase student diversity within and between public and private schools, given the regulations governing the plan (Arsen, Plank, & Sykes, 1999; Frankenberg & Lee, 2003; Whitty, 1997). Others argue that since many urban schools are already segregated, more choice is not likely to further segregate them and that families of color deserve more choices than represented by the public schools attended by their children (Arons, 1989; Barnes, 1997; Smith, 1996). Some school choice plans—such as charter schools in select states—allow for the selection and recruitment of students by gender, ability, or academic interest so as to meet a particular pedagogical need (Schnaiberg, 2000; Wells, Lopez, Scott, & Jellison-Holme, 1999).

In comparison, the express purpose of some choice plans is to preserve or maintain diversity, such as in magnet schools or controlled choice programs (Fiske & Ladd, 2000; Fuller et al., 1996; Glatter, Woods, & Bagley, 1997; B. Levin, 1999; Willie, Edwards, & Alves, 2002). The adoption of any given school choice plan, then, without express attention to diversity, is unlikely to increase the integration of students in terms of race, class, linguistics, gender, or ability.

## THE INTERACTION OF SCHOOL CHOICE AND RACIAL DESEGREGATION

Of the categories into which students are segregated, that of race remains the most intractable, and it is also one of the primary indicators parents use to choose a "good" school when choice of school is available (see, for example, Chapter 1). Finding barometers for measuring school "goodness" has become an increasing concern of parents as high-stakes accountability measures, such as the No Child Left Behind legislation, result in schools being affixed with achievement labels and low-performing schools being threatened with sanctions and closures. Even well-intentioned parents have little incentive to choose a school in which large numbers of children of color or high-poverty students are enrolled.

Policymakers and advocates continue to expand school choice through federal, state, and local initiatives and raise the stakes of accountability and testing at the same time as courts are increasingly limiting and, at times, terminating race-based school desegregation plans.

Throughout the 1990s, and into the 21st century, two dominant educational policy trends have thrived and, in many ways, intersected. The first is the granting of unitary status by the courts to school districts around the country, enabling districts to cease affirmative efforts to desegregate schools racially. Court-ordered school integration plans have ended in landmark sites, including Charlotte, NC, Louisville, KY, and Norfolk, VA (Frankenberg & Lee, 2002; B. Fuller et al., 1996; Orfield, 2001). As a result of these court decisions and the shifting demographic patterns of suburban communities, many urban school systems have become resegregated (Orfield & Eaton, 1996). Thus, intradistrict racial and socioeconomic segregation, as well as segregation between city and suburban school systems, has flourished (Frankenberg & Lee, 2002; Orfield & Eaton, 1996). Meanwhile, notions of diversity have greatly expanded to include consideration of gender, ability, and language, even as race continues to figure prominently in parental choices (Wells & Serna, 1996).

As school systems become increasingly segregated, the second dominant trend in educational policy and politics has been the rapid expansion of school choice options, including charter schools, publicly and privately funded vouchers, open-enrollment plans, tuition tax credits, and magnet schools. According to the Education Commission of the

States, by 2004 at least one form of school choice policy existed in every U.S. state except Alabama. The recent U.S. Supreme Court ruling in *Zelman v. Simmons-Harris* (2002) upholding the constitutionality of Cleveland's voucher program has caused other states to consider implementing similar plans. The Bush administration's educational-reform legislation, No Child Left Behind, provides for public school choices for students in schools that have been identified as failing. Thus, individual states and the federal government are encouraging the expansion of choice at the very time that options for increasing student diversity—particularly racial diversity—are being narrowed by the courts.

## DEBATING THE VALUE OF STUDENT DIVERSITY

Meanwhile, the value of student diversity is being questioned in some communities. Indeed, the value of racial integration versus separation has been debated among African Americans since shortly after Emancipation (Du Bois, 1935; Tyack, 1974). More recently, some advocates and parents in communities of color have suggested that the pursuit of diversity without sufficient concern for the treatment of children of color in diverse institutions or attention to academic quality has in fact resulted in poor academic and social outcomes for children of color (Farkas, Johnson, Immerwahr, & McHugh, 1998; Holt, 2000; Shujaa, 1993).

In urban school districts, where African American and Latino students often make up the majority—and in some cases the entirety—of the student population, some of their parents have grown weary of efforts to integrate these students with the few White students who remain, especially in light of high-stakes accountability measures on which their children fall woefully behind. They have joined with school choice advocates to create choices within city boundaries that include taxpayer and privately funded vouchers for private and religious schools (Apple, 2002; Carl, 1996; H. Fuller, 2000).

In other cases, charter schools have been started to serve specific marginalized populations such as girls, Native Americans, disabled students, and English-language learners. The concept of diversity is by no means universally accepted as an educational good, especially in contexts in which many children and their communities were harmed by poorly implemented school desegregation plans.

At the same time, even as Americans commemorated the 50th anniversary of the *Brown v. Board of Education* ruling in 2004, desegregation—if not full integration—continues to be an enduring yet elusive goal for public and many private institutions. The spirit of *Brown*—the notion that student diversity is a valuable public-policy goal and that separate institutions are inherently unequal—still holds political and moral currency, even as the promise of *Brown* (education for all on equal terms) is constrained by limited educational choices and resources for students, teachers, and families. Longitudinal research reveals many positive attributes of desegregated schooling: students who attend schools with diverse student bodies are more likely to attend integrated universities, work in diverse settings, and choose to live in integrated neighborhoods (Braddock, Crain, & McPartland, 1984; Braddock & McPartland, 1988; Wells & Crain, 1994). Despite these benefits of diversity in schooling, many choice plans being offered do not have provisions that encourage it to flourish.

Current choice plans often limit choices for urban students to only those schools found within the city boundaries (Ryan & Heise, 2002). For example, in the Cleveland voucher program upheld by the Supreme Court in the *Zelman* ruling, though students were eligible to choose public schools in the well-resourced surrounding suburbs, not a single suburban district chose to participate (Metcalf, 2001). As a result, Cleveland students seeking educational choices with diversity have few options. Even urban private and parochial schools are increasingly made up of students of color, often almost exclusively African American and Latino students from poor and working-class families. Like their public counterparts, these schools tend to have fewer resources, fewer high-quality teachers, and lower levels of academic achievement as measured by standardized tests (Rothstein, Carnoy, & Benveniste, 1999).

Parental preferences—which are based on a variety of factors, including race and social class—housing patterns influenced by the legacy of state-sponsored segregation, new immigration, and pedagogical concerns, all make the practice of shaping diverse school communities while also increasing school choice options inordinately complex (Massey & Denton, 1993).

## ORGANIZATION OF THE COLLECTION

The authors in this collection engage and tease out this complexity. They consider the conditions under which school choice can increase or diminish student diversity, doing so from a number of methodological approaches and conceptual orientations. This volume joins the growing literature on school choice that addresses choice plans within a social context (B. Fuller, 2000; Rasell & Rothstein, 1993; Sugarman & Kemerer, 1999). All school choice reforms, however, are embedded in particular social, economic, and legal contexts and thus intersect with student diversity in a variety of ways.

The writers in this collection examine the relationship between educational polices that purport to give more choices to parents, students, and schools and the effect such choice policies have on student diversity. This book bridges some chasms in the debates among educational researchers and policymakers with regard to issues of race, social class, special education, and gender. It brings together a collection of empirical and theoretical research to consider the question, Under which contexts and conditions does school choice increase or decrease student diversity?

There are two sections to the book. The authors in the first section consider the factors parents use when making choices about schools or housing. In Chapter 1, Hamilton Lankford and James Wyckoff, use data from the 1990 Census of Population and Housing to examine the relationship between the choice of public and private schooling and school characteristics such as race or educational inputs. They find that White families leave urban public schools in reaction to large enrollments of minority students. Chapter 2 is by Jay Greene, an advocate of expanded school choice. Greene finds that the literature fails to capture important nuances of why parents may choose private schools. He presents a proposal for conceptualizing and measuring integration. In Chapter 3, John Yun and Sean Reardon look at diversity within private schools and find that this sector shows similar patterns of segregation to those of the public schools. They speculate that expanded school choice is unlikely to diversify private schools.

The contributors in the second section of the book turn to specific school choice plans. In this section, the authors present findings on what happens to student diversity when these plans are implemented. Chapter 4, by Amy Stuart Wells and Robert Crain, examines various school choice and controlled choice school integration plans. The authors conclude that these plans present attempts to balance parental choice with the public goals of integration and equity. In Chapter 5, Carol Ascher and Nathalis Wamba lay a foundation for examining equity in charter schools. After considering a variety of standards, the authors propose their own standard for equity, one that is based on student outcomes. Following this, Kevin Welner and Kenneth Howe, in Chapter 6, consider the practice engaged in by some charter schools of steering away special education students. In Chapter 7, Amanda Datnow, Lea Hubbard, and Elisabeth Woody examine single-gender academies. These were magnet schools offering distinct curricular foci. The authors found that the schools attracted the racial and ethnic student populations they did because of the targeted educational programs they offered. Finally, in

Chapter 8, Roslyn Arlin Mickelson provides an analysis of the resegrega-tion of the Charlotte-Mecklenburg school system once a school choice plan replaced the district's desegregation plan.

Together, the sections of the book can be of help to policymakers and public school officials who are interested in both multiplying paren-tal choices and protecting equal access to public schooling and who wish to design better choice options. The chapters indicate that a better under-standing of the choice processes of parents, and of how political, social, and economic contexts shape such choices, can help officials design choice plans to encourage greater diversity or to preserve the diversity that already exists. It may be possible to achieve student diversity even as parental preferences for meaningful choices in schooling abound, but diversity will not be achieved without a consideration of the contexts within which parents, teachers, and students make choices and of the subsequent crafting of balanced school choice plans.

# Chapter 1

# Why Are Schools Racially Segregated?

## *Implications for School Choice Policies*

### HAMILTON LANKFORD and JAMES WYCKOFF

A striking feature of the U.S. K–12 educational system is the pronounced racial, economic, and social segregation of students. Low-income, high-needs, and minority children are concentrated in urban centers, while higher-income, better-educated, White families are typically found in the suburbs and private schools. However, because stratification can result from a variety of factors, these patterns are not well understood. For example, if parents who are typically higher income, better-educated, and also disproportionately White tend to believe that suburban and private schools are better, then schools become racially stratified. In this case, providing urban schools with the resources to attract better school inputs would reduce stratification. However, if high-income, well-educated White parents want only that their children be educated with similar children, then improving school inputs would have little effect on stratification.

The debate over expanded school choice offers a good example of this confusion. Student stratification, especially racial segregation, is often debated in proposals to expand school choice (Chubb & Moe, 1990; Finn, 1991). This debate suffers from two problems. First, it is often ideological, without much, if any, reference to the growing empirically-based literature on factors affecting parents' schooling decisions. Second, it is frequently a rather sterile depiction of choice as either existing or absent. Important forms of choice exist within the current educational system, and expanded choice could take a variety of forms that have important nuances. As with most interesting policy questions, a richer understanding of behavior may allow for policy designs that achieve multiple policy goals.

In this chapter, we explore the linkages between the choices that parents make regarding the schools their children attend and the racial segregation of students. Our data is from metropolitan areas in upstate New York. Most of the analysis examines this relationship within the context of choice through residential location and choice between the public and private sectors. The analysis considers choice within these parameters since the existing system is heavily segregated and since many of the contextual factors that lead to segregation will likely continue in the face of expanded school choice.

We find that White parents' preference to have their children educated in schools that have lower concentrations of non-Whites is the dominant—though not exclusive factor—leading to racial segregation of students in metropolitan areas. This result occurs across a variety of model specifications. The extent to which White and minority students attend a school is directly related to the racial composition of the school. White families' racial preferences have important implications for the design of school choice policies whose goals include a reduction of racial segregation.

After summarizing the extent of the racial, economic, and social stratification of students within the current education system, we outline alternative explanations for how such stratification can arise. We then present empirical findings that speak to the relative importance of these explanations. Finally, we explore the implications of our findings with respect to expanded school choice.

## INCREASING RACIAL SEGREGATION

Following the 1954 Supreme Court desegregation ruling in *Brown v. Topeka Board of Education* and beginning in earnest with the civil rights movement in the mid-1960s, the United States embarked on a sustained effort to address issues of racial segregation in elementary and secondary schools. Although the causes of segregation varied, desegregation efforts resulted in substantial reductions in racial segregation within school districts.

Racial segregation in public schools fell dramatically from 1968 until the early 1970s and remained constant throughout the remainder of the 1970s; it has increased slightly since then (Orfield, 1983; Boozer, Kreuger, & Wolkon, 1992). However, this overall trend masks increases in segregation in northeastern public schools, which were more segregated in 1989 than they were in 1968 and were more segregated than in any other region of the country. Rivkin (1994) and Clotfelter (1999) find that virtually all the racial segregation that currently exists in public schools results from the location decisions of households among school districts and not from insufficient efforts to integrate schools within districts. Orfield (1994) argues that the relatively large numbers of small school districts in northeastern metropolitan areas allow families to more easily choose to live in communities that provide desired social services. Reflecting the 1974 ruling by the U.S. Supreme Court in *Milliken v. Bradley* that interdistrict desegregation plans were not permitted, the increasing between-district segregation of students has continued unimpeded by public policy (Clotfelter, 2001).

Student racial segregation in New York state is illustrative of the trends in the northeast. Upstate New York elementary schools were substantially more segregated in 1995 than they were in 1970. Overall segregation doubled during this 25-year period (see Lankford and Wyckoff, 1999). Even more provocative is the changing pattern of segregation in schools. When the inequality is decomposed into that which occurs within individual sectors (here defined as urban public schools, suburban public schools and private schools) and that which occurs between sectors, more than 60% of the total racial segregation in 1970 was within urban public school districts. By 1995, segregation within urban public school districts accounted for less than a quarter of all segregation. Virtually all the growth in segregation during this period occurred in the between-sector component. In 1970, racial segregation in upstate New York metropolitan elementary schools was largely attributable to segregated residential location patterns *within* districts. By 1995, Whites increasingly were opting out of urban districts and locating in suburban districts. As a result, segregation in schools is increasingly attributable to residential location patterns *between* districts. The proportion of all White students attending urban public schools fell between 1970 and 1995 by a third, while the total number of White students declined by 36%. The proportion of African American and Latino students enrolled in urban public schools remained unchanged, while the total number of black and Latino students increased by 30%. Reflecting these trends, the proportion of urban public school students who were African American or Latino doubled. Over the period, the racial composition of suburban public schools changed little. This pattern is consistent with the findings of Massey and Hazal (1995) that residential segregation between jurisdictions has increased.

We now turn to a discussion of the processes that might have caused the striking and increasing level of racial segregation.

## EXPLANATIONS FOR INCREASED RACIAL SEGREGATION

The existing stratification of students is the result of the interplay between the institutional features of the educational system, the attributes of the educational environment, and the educational choices made by families. Various institutional features affect the scope and nature of choice within the educational system that, in turn, affect the school choices made by parents. These choices in the aggregate feed back to alter the school choice environment in a variety of ways.

Three related institutional features help shape the educational environment so that segregation can occur. First, households in metropolitan areas have a large number of schooling options from which to choose. Most metropolitan areas have many public school districts, each with multiple schooling options; in addition, private schools offer a variety of educational alternatives. Second, public school choices are usually defined by residential location. Few metropolitan areas offer multidistrict school choice and most districts still employ neighborhood attendance (i.e., catchment) areas to determine the public school each child attends. Finally, the public school systems in most states rely heavily on local governance, production, and finance. Taken together, these institutional features lead to a school choice environment that has the potential to exhibit wide variations in student diversity. However, public-private school choice and residential location remain the primary means by which parents exercise choice.

Residential location and public-private school choice will depend upon the attributes of the available school alternatives, including the quantity and quality of purchased inputs (e.g., teachers), educational orientation, and student-body composition. The potential importance of "social inputs" follows from the interactive nature of the educational process. In particular, a student's educational attainment could be affected by the abilities, motivation, and attitudes of other students. Such factors—often called peer-group effects, neighborhood effects, or social capital—have been the focus of extensive research in sociology, psychology, and economics. Questions remain regarding the magnitudes and nature of such peer effects (Manski, 1993). However, if parents perceive educational outcomes as depending upon the attributes of student peers, their assessments of alternative school options will depend upon those student-body attributes that they perceive to be important. Independent of any link between educational outcomes and student-body composition, parents also might have preferences in the racial, economic, or social attributes of their child's peers.

Important questions arise regarding how parents assess school quality and what information they employ in making school choices. Facing the daunting task of trying to understand how educational inputs differ across schools and how these inputs affect educational outcomes, parents might well use easily observed proxies for school quality. These might include student-body attributes, based on views such as "the school must be of high quality since so many well-educated professionals have chosen it for their children." Even if parents use mean student test scores or college-going rates to proxy school quality, the result will be similar given the high correlation between such outcomes and various student-body attributes.

Whether because of peer effects, preferences for association, or parents' using student-based proxies for educational quality, student composition could be of direct concern to parents, possibly even more important than the quantity and quality of purchased inputs. If student-body attributes affect the school choices of individual parents, the result will be a dynamic process in which student-body attributes affect school choices, which in turn affect the composition of students in schools. As discussed by Schelling (1971) and Clotfelter (1976), this can have an effect that amplifies the importance of student-body attributes. Racial segregation could result merely from the concerns of parents regarding nonracial attributes of student peers. This dynamic process is important in understanding how the school choices of parents could affect the racial composition of schools.

Other feedbacks are pertinent as well. For example, differences in the quality of public schools will likely lead to residential sorting. In addition to any direct effects associated with changes in student-body composition, there could well be other effects through the political process. For example, those willing to pay more for higher-quality schools may segregate themselves into communities in such a way that cause local public education funding to increase, further improving school quality. This along with a reversed pattern of change in lower-quality schools is potentially important in understanding why there is such a range in the educational opportunities available to students.

Even though preferences for association, peer-group effects, and the use of student-body attributes to proxy quality can all lead to stratification, it is important to recognize that none of these explanations are necessary for complete stratification to occur. Other factors result in a natural tendency toward stratification. Consider the typical case in which the range of educational alternatives is such that better schools have higher costs to parents. Private school tuition is one such cost, but many others accrue to both public and private school attendance, depending on the institutional structure. If families differ either in their ability or their willingness to pay for educational quality, children of those willing to pay more will be sorted into better-quality schools, and those having relatively lower willingness or ability to pay will attend lower-quality schools. Thus, to the extent that families differ in their ability or willingness to pay for education quality and this is correlated with their race, the school choices made by parents will result in racial sorting.

The observed stratification of students may be in part the result of factors not directly related to school choice decisions. Where families choose to live will depend upon a range of other factors, including proximity to work, costs of housing, and quality of local amenities other than education. To the extent that these and other factors, such as housing discrimination, lead to residential segregation, the result will be a corresponding segregation of students resulting from the use of residential location to define public school attendance.

In summary, parents' assessments of schools can depend upon various purchased inputs, peer inputs, student-body socioeconomic attributes independent of their effects on educational quality, and school racial composition. As long as minority families and White families differ in their demands for any of these attributes, the ability of most families to choose from a large menu of public and private schools with varying levels of each of these attributes will lead to racial sorting. These factors are not mutually exclusive. Indeed, decisions regarding the education of their children may well be affected by several of these explanations. It is the net effect of each of these arguments in conjunction with the individual attributes of minority and White parents that will determine the racial segregation of schools.

The existing stratification of students within the current educational system is a reflection of the educational choices made by families of school-age children. Institutional features will place limits on and influence those choices. However, within any institutional setting, understanding the factors driving the school choices of individual parents is crucial to understanding the root causes of economic, social, and racial stratification.

Even if one accepts this characterization of the school choice environment and the channels through which economic, social, and racial stratification could occur, a central question remains: What is the empirical importance of each of these potential explanations? A better understanding of this question will bring some clarity to the discussion of how expanding school choice would affect educational choices of parents and, in turn, the segregation of students. We now discuss empirical data that indicate that the racial makeup of a school's student body is the dominant factor in parental choices of schooling.

## EMPIRICAL EVIDENCE

To examine the relative importance of the numerous factors potentially influencing the racial segregation of schools, we examine the school choices that parents make within the current system. As described earlier, the school a child attends results from choices parents make regarding residential location and public-private school choice. Our analysis of these decisions in upstate New York is based on data that thoroughly defines the characteristics of parents and their children, as well as the attributes of schools.

### Data

We have constructed a household-level data set for eight metropolitan areas in upstate New York. Student and family data are linked to detailed information regarding the full set of schools and residential locations from which the families choose. We focus on metropolitan areas because opportunities for school and residential location choices are greatest in these areas and advocates of greater choice often cite education in urban areas as the largest beneficiary of choice. New York was chosen because detailed information is available for both public and private schools and because metropolitan areas in New York are composed of many—typically 20 or more—public school districts. In such a setting individuals are presented with a large choice set from which to select residences and schools, allowing us to better understand the factors that are important in their decisions.

Household-level data are drawn from the sample of households completing the 1990 Census of Population and Housing long form, which includes information on whether each child attended public or private school. We were able to identify the census block of residence for each household using restricted-access files at the Bureau of the Census. The public school district for each residential location was then determined by means of a geographical mapping file that maps census blocks into political jurisdictions (e.g., public school districts).

In contrast to the relatively small, homogeneous suburban school districts, urban districts typically are quite large. Because of significant intradistrict differences between urban public schools, district-level statistics are likely to be poor proxies for the local urban public school attributes that are relevant in both the public-private school and location choices of families. Such intradistrict variation motivated our mapping urban census blocks into individual public school attendance areas. A complication arises when public school districts do not use neighborhood school attendance boundaries exclusively to determine enrollment (e.g., magnet schools). Because of the complexity of the public choice environment and the fact that nearly all students attend neighborhood schools, we choose to model the local public school option as the school for the neighborhood attendance area.

In this way, our analysis of public-private school choice is based upon information regarding the exact urban public school alternative available to each student. The elementary school catchment areas are also used to represent the elemental "residential communities" within the set of urban localities. Supporting this decision, Orfield (1994) argues that school attendance areas are useful in delineating neighborhoods, providing a sharper focus than the census tracts that are typically employed in residential location research.

Census data only indicate whether each student attends public or private school; there is no information for those attending private school regarding the particular private school, or type of private school, attended. However, we are able to obtain aggregate data from the New York Department of Education on the number of students living in each public school district that attend *each* private school. Similar data disaggregated to public school attendance areas were obtained for the city districts of Rochester and Syracuse. These aggregate data on private school enrollments are used along with school and census data to estimate a model of private school choice.

Metropolitan areas were defined as including urban public school districts and suburban districts in a two-district ring around the urban district(s). Table 1.1 enumerates the school choices available to parents in each of our eight metropolitan areas. In each metropolitan area parents have a large number of private and public school alternatives from which to choose. There are more than 30 private elementary schools and

**Table 1.1.** Available Private Elementary Schools and Residential Location Options by Metropolitan Area

| | Number of Private Elementary Schools by Category | | | | Residential Communities | |
|---|---|---|---|---|---|---|
| | Baptist-Fundamentalist | Catholic | Other Religious | Independent | Urban | Suburban |
| Albany–Schenectady–Troy | 9 | 40 | 4 | 7 | 29 | 30 |
| Binghamton | 5 | 12 | 2 | 1 | 7 | 11 |
| Elmira | 9 | 6 | 1 | 1 | 9 | 6 |
| Jamestown-Dunkirk | 5 | 3 | 5 | 0 | 11 | 13 |
| Poughkeepsie | 5 | 14 | 3 | 5 | 4 | 8 |
| Rochester | 19 | 45 | 9 | 6 | 33 | 25 |
| Syracuse | 7 | 29 | 2 | 2 | 24 | 22 |
| Utica-Rome | 3 | 18 | 1 | 2 | 27 | 21 |
| Metropolitan average | 7.75 | 20.88 | 3.38 | 3.0 | 18.0 | 17.0 |

35 public elementary school options in the average metropolitan area in our sample.

## Empirical Model

The central focus of the following empirical analysis concerns how the school choices made by parents for their children are affected by the race of the parents, the quantity and quality of purchased school inputs, and student-body attributes. The results presented are drawn from a general empirical model of school choice that accounts for school choice through residential location, public-private school choice, and, for those choosing the private sector, the choice of particular private schools. We have estimated the behavioral model to gain a better understanding of the causes and consequences of choice within the current educational system as well as the consequences of institutional reforms to increase opportunities for choice.

Very often, empirical analyses of choice are descriptive in nature, summarizing who chooses various school alternatives and the attributes of the schools attended or not attended. These analyses typically are not sufficient to allow one to infer the underlying behavioral relationships.

To identify these determinants of choice, an analysis must account for the full set of choices available to families as well as the range of pertinent attributes characterizing the individual public and private school alternatives that are important to the parents making those choices. This characterization of schools needs to include a rich set of variables measuring the quantity and quality of purchased inputs as well as various aspects of the students in each school. Without such a full set of variables, it is not possible to infer the direct effects of individual school attributes. If only a subset of the relevant school attributes is included, the estimated effect of any included variable merely could reflect the direct effect of some omitted variable.

Our empirical model makes two important advances over past research. First, the model accounts for the important school choices available to parents within the current educational system—both residential location and public private school choice. Second, the data characterizing the individual school alternatives are far richer than the types of data employed in past research, including our own work. These features are important as we seek to isolate the attributes of school and families that are the key behavioral determinants of school choice.

Even though the following discussion focuses on how public school and family attributes affect the decision whether to attend public or private school, it is important to remember that this submodel is part of our broader analysis of school choice. The factors affecting public-private school choice are the same as those affecting school choice through residential location. We focus on the former because the choice is closer in nature to the types of expanded choice envisioned by choice proponents. However, even though the discussion is in terms of public-private school choice, the central question concerns how school and family attributes affect the school choices of parents generally—even under altered choice environments.

### Modeling How Parents Choose Schools

The ways in which various school and family attributes affect the school choices made by parents could differ depending upon their own race or educational attainment. To investigate this possibility, we estimate separate school-choice models for subsamples of students based on race and whether at least one parent had a college education (for a fuller description of the empirical model, estimation strategy, and results, see Lankford and Wyckoff, 1999). Results indicate that there are systematic differences related to parental education. For example, we find that teacher quality, measured by the selectivity of the colleges they attend, and student-peer attributes, measured by the proportion of public-school students having a college-educated parent, are relatively more important to college-educated parents in their assessments of schools than is the case for less well educated parents. As discussed below, we also find large systematic differences between minority and White parents in how the racial composition of schools affects their school choices. However, other than in this important exception, the effects of school and other personal attributes appear to be similar for minority and White parents. The model allows the effect of school racial composition to differ with the race of parents and allows the effects of all variables to differ with whether a parent has a college education (for a discussion of similar findings in Chile, see McEwan and Carnoy, 1998). Unless otherwise noted, the empirical results discussed below are in reference to this specification.

Probabilities for a student must be considered in reference to a particular public school setting and set of personal attributes. We investigate how each variable affects the school choice probability, changing the variables one at a time while holding all other variables at their default levels. Reflecting our interest in school choice within urban areas, the estimated probabilities are for the default case in which all public school attributes are evaluated at the means for urban public schools.

The (estimated) likelihood of attending private school varies with a parent's own educational attainment. Most of the change in likelihood is associated with whether the parent has a college, as opposed to a high school, education. For a minority student having other attributes typical of minority students residing in urban centers, the probability that the student opts for a private school alternative ranges from 0.047 for a parent not having a high school degree to 0.185 for a college-educated parent. The probability change for a representative White urban student is even larger.

As expected, being Catholic reduces the probability of attending public school. The estimated effect for the typical White student is large, representing a 50% increase in the likelihood that the student attends private school. Even though the change for the minority student is substantially smaller, the percentage *increase* in the likelihood of attending private school is actually larger.

The qualitative effects of occupation type, marital status and family income are as one would expect. Higher-income, married, and white-collar parents are more likely to send their children to private school, other things equal. Individually, these effects are smaller than that of parent education. For example, for a college-educated White parent the difference associated with being a white-collar worker is only a fifth as large that associated with the change in education. However, one should not dismiss the importance of these variables. First, the absolute changes are meaningful. For example, the increase in the probability of choosing a private alternative associated with being married is estimated to be 0.043. The probability that a child in a single-parent household attends private school is 0.198. Relative to being in a two-parent home this equates to a 17% difference. Second, even if the individual effects are not large, such variables as a group can have a large effect.

Several other family attributes are estimated to have statistically significant effects. The estimated effects of one's own race require some additional explanation. We have calculated the probabilities with all school attributes evaluated at the means for urban public schools in our sample. In this case, the probability of an African American or Latino student attending private school is estimated to be 0.071. This contrasts to 0.141 for an otherwise identical White student. In the case of students having nonrace attributes like those of a typical urban White student, the effect of one's own race is even larger. The White parent is almost twice as likely to opt for the private school alternative as an otherwise identical minority parent.

Systematic differences between minority and white parents, holding all school and other personal attributes constant, will contribute directly to racial segregation. In addition, other parental attributes will have indirect effects. This follows from the effects of parent education, income, occupation, religion, and marital status discussed above and the fact that these attributes differ systematically across racial groups. As shown in the first two columns of Table 1.2, White parents on average have higher incomes and more education and are more likely to be Catholic, married, and employed in white-collar jobs. The large differences in these variables, together with the effects these variables have on school choice, work to exacerbate the differences in the school choice probabilities for minority and White students resulting from the direct effect of race.

It is interesting to compare the relative importance of the direct and indirect effects. The estimated probability that a minority student, having family attributes equal to the mean attributes for all urban minority students (including the racial composition of the school), will attend private school is 0.071. In contrast, the probability for a White student having family attributes equal to the means for all urban White students is estimated to be 0.228. The estimated probability of a minority student attending private school goes from 0.071 to 0.119 when all the nonrace student and family attributes change from the mean values for urban minority students to those for urban White students. This (indirect) probability change for a minority student, resulting from nonrace socio-

**Table 1.2.** Descriptive Statistics

| Individual Attributes | All minority students (1) | All White students (2) | Students not having a college-educated parent | | Students having one or more college-educated parent | |
|---|---|---|---|---|---|---|
| | | | Minority (5) | White (6) | Minority (7) | White (8) |
| Minority | 1.000 | 0.000 | 1.000 | 0.000 | 1.000 | 0.000 |
| College graduate | 0.085 | 0.246 | 0.000 | 0.000 | 1.000 | 1.000 |
| High school graduate | 0.704 | 0.871 | 0.677 | 0.829 | 1.000 | 1.000 |
| Income | $25,844 | $35,870 | $23,654 | $29,387 | $49,532 | $55,740 |
| White-collar | 0.416 | 0.645 | 0.370 | 0.551 | 0.919 | 0.932 |
| Blue-collar | 0.466 | 0.303 | 0.501 | 0.382 | 0.081 | 0.062 |
| Married | 0.447 | 0.723 | 0.424 | 0.669 | 0.696 | 0.891 |
| Catholic | 0.198 | 0.374 | 0.196 | 0.379 | 0.219 | 0.362 |
| Baptist | 0.463 | 0.177 | 0.466 | 0.178 | 0.424 | 0.176 |
| Jewish | 0.003 | 0.025 | 0.003 | 0.022 | 0.001 | 0.035 |

economic differences between White and minority students, is approximately a third of the total change. Alternatively, the (indirect) probability change for a White student, resulting from the nonrace socioeconomic differences, is slightly more than half of the total change. It is clear that roughly a half to two thirds of the total probability difference is the result of the direct effect of race, with the remainder caused by the indirect effects of all other family attributes.

When considering issues of racial sorting, it is the overall difference in the probability of attending the private alternative that is of central importance. From this perspective, we find a "typical" urban White student to be over three times as likely to opt out of the local public school alternative as the "typical" urban minority student. Such systematic sorting—holding public school attributes constant—is important. A disproportionately larger number of White parents opting out of the local public school alternative will result in those remaining being disproportionately minority.

Our empirical results provide strong evidence that interactions between personal and school attributes are important in determining how parents evaluate school alternatives. One such finding is that parents who are college educated value certain school attributes (e.g., the educational attainment of teachers) more highly than do less educated parents. We also find an important interaction between a parent's own race and the racial composition of a school. The probabilities associated with one's own race differ with alternative values of the school racial composition, holding all other school attributes at the means for urban public schools. The probability of an urban White student's attending a private school is 0.143 when the proportion of minorities in the public school equals 0.10 and is 0.209 when that proportion increases to 0.30. In the case of an otherwise similar minority student, the estimated probability of attending a private school changes little in response to an equal change in the proportion of the student body that is minority. Even though changes in school racial composition have very little effect on the school choices of minority parents, the effects for Whites are substantial. These findings are consistent with those of other researchers who find that Whites are less likely to choose schools having higher percentages of minority students (Clotfelter, 2001; Conlon & Kimenyi, 1991; Cready & Fossett, 1998; Glazerman, 1998; Goldhaber, 1996; Lankford & Wyckoff, 1992, 1995; Saporito & Lareau, 1999; Yancey & Saporito, 1995).

Just as the interaction between a parent's own race and the racial composition of a school has implications for how the school choices of parents are affected by changes in school racial composition, the interaction affects how school-choice probabilities differ with the race of the parent, holding school racial composition constant. When only a small percentage of students in a public school are African American or Latino, White and minority students who are otherwise identical have very similar probabilities of remaining in the school. However, the reaction of White parents to school racial composition results in these probabilities diverging as minority students make up an increasing portion of the student body. In short, the extent to which White and minority students differ in their propensity to attend a particular school largely depends upon the racial composition of the school. This finding is important in understanding why school choices often differ for White and minority students.

There are other important interactions between the characteristics of schools and the attributes of parents making school choices. For example, teacher quality, measured by the selectivity of the colleges the teachers attended, is relatively more important to college-educated parents in their assessments of schools than to less well educated parents. The same is true for the importance of student-body characteristics, proxied by the proportion of public school students having a college-educated parent. Such interactions are important in understanding how parent attributes affect school choices, as well as how changes in school attributes affect the school choices of different types of parents.

## PUBLIC-PRIVATE SUMMARY

Our research provides information on the behavioral factors that underlie racial segregation in schools. We find that Whites are much more likely to leave public schools than are minorities. This results from a combination of effects. Much of it reflects the different reaction that Whites have to a given set of school attributes, holding their individual attributes constant. In particular, Whites are much more likely to exit public schools as the proportion of minority students in public schools increases.

Whites also react to changes in the other attributes of their student peers more strongly than do minorities. Both minorities and Whites respond positively to the quality of public schools as represented by purchased inputs. Finally, differences between minorities and whites in individual attributes (e.g., their education, income, and religion) are also important. However, controlling for these attributes, the race of the individual does not affect school choice with the important exception that White parents react strongly to the racial composition of schools, as noted above.

### Residential Location

As one way of documenting the generality of these public-private results, we briefly report our research that examines residential location decisions (Lankford & Wycoff, 1999). Given neighborhood catchment, residential location allows parents to select from among the many public schools that exist within most metropolitan areas. The residential-location empirical model includes a variety of variables that characterize the options families consider when making location decisions, including attributes of the individuals, housing stock, characteristics of the educational options, and other local government attributes. We find that those variables that are important in the public-private school choice model are also important in determining locational choices. The importance of school variables is shown in the following. If urban public schools had attributes like those of their suburban counterparts, the proportion of families living in owner-occupied housing who would reside in urban areas and send their children to public school would be three times as large, when compared to a situation in which these families were confronted with the actual attributes of urban schools.

The racial composition of schools and neighborhoods is the dominant factor explaining the change in residential location, as shown in the following thought experiment. Instead of changing all the urban school attributes to those of suburban schools, as was done above, change only the racial composition of urban schools to those of suburban schools, leaving the other school attributes set to their urban values. When this is done, 70% of the overall increase in urban residential location and public school attendance results from merely changing the racial composition of urban public schools.

In general, the results for residential location are consistent with those from the public-private school choice analysis. Parents express many of the same preferences in choosing from among their public school options via residential location as they do when considering the choice between public and private schools. This supports our belief that the preferences that are manifest in making public–private school choice decisions will emerge when other forms of choice are considered.

We believe that these patterns will hold as other forms of school choice are examined because they reveal important aspects of preferences that are likely independent of the specific institutional structure of choice. Although enhanced school choice, such as the voucher plans currently being explored in a few urban school districts, undoubtedly change the feasible choices for many families, they probably do not alter underlying preferences. As demonstrated earlier, it is these preferences that play an important role in explaining current patterns of segregation.

## IMPLICATIONS FOR ENHANCED SCHOOL CHOICE

This understanding of the factors affecting whether parents opt out of public schools has important implications for understanding new forms of enhanced school choice. Enhanced school choice holds substantial promise in improving educational outcomes, especially for the large number of students in urban areas. One of the distinct advantages of many choice plans is the potential to break the link between school attendance and residential location. If improved racial integration is a social goal of enhanced choice, then breaking the connection between place of residence and place of schooling offers poor minority families access to better-quality schools. Doing so could lead to less segregated housing patterns. However, the results presented above lead us to be cautious about the design of school choice plans because we believe that there is too much racial segregation in the current system, and enhanced choice could lead to further segregation, depending on the design of the plan.

We have two major concerns. First, White families have strong preferences to avoid minorities and socioeconomic attributes correlated with minorities. As such, any plan that makes school choice more accessible to Whites will likely increase segregation, unless the plan also includes policies that constrain or countervail this behavior. So-called controlled choice plans offer a direct constraint on further segregation. These plans require that any movement of students must make segregation no worse. Alternatively, enhanced choice could be targeted to low-income families. This would mean that minorities would disproportionately benefit and might well induce increased integration, as minorities are attracted to schools with higher-quality purchased inputs and stronger student peers. The ultimate test would include the racial composition of the entire metropolitan area. It may well be that a choice plan draws Whites from suburban schools to urban environments that are more heavily minority. This would provide strong support for the benefits of such a plan with respect to segregation. However, given the strong preferences of Whites, merely offering minorities better access may not improve integration, as this altered environment will have important feedback effects on the decisions of Whites.

Our second concern relates to the political economy of public school resource allocations. Many choice plans effectively reduce the resources that are available to urban public schools. Many charter school and public school choice or open-enrollment plans have this character. Reducing urban public school resources will likely lead to a reduction in purchased inputs, which in turn reduce the attractiveness of these schools, especially to Whites, resulting in increased segregation. There may be good reasons to allow the market to move resources away from nonperforming schools, but it nonetheless will likely increase segregation.

Is there any promise for reducing racial segregation? Our results suggest that variables under the control of policymakers can reduce the probability of Whites' opting out of public schools. For example, the strong preferences by both Whites and minorities for high-quality purchased inputs create an opportunity to reduce segregation. Policies that redistribute or target resources to urban school districts to reduce class size or improve the educational credentials of teachers will induce the strongest response by Whites to remain in urban public schools. Thus within-district public school choice plans and magnet schools that provide net additional resources for the quantity and quality of teachers offer a vehicle to reduce or reverse the movement of whites to suburban and private schools and therefore improve the racial composition of schools in metropolitan areas.

School choice plans can be designed in a variety of ways to achieve multiple policy goals. If racial integration of students is one of these goals, then the design of school choice plans should account for the underlying preferences of minorities and Whites for the various dimensions of education described in this chapter. Failure to do so ignores the behavior that has led to the current highly segregated system, behavior that will likely emerge in other choice settings.

## NOTE

The research assistance of Michael Collins, Frank Papa, and Lester Rhee, as well as the assistance of officials in each of the urban districts, is greatly appreciated.

Chapter 2

# Choosing Integration

JAY P. GREENE

Research and policy discussion on parental choice and school integration is muddled by confusion about how to conceptualize and measure integration. Before discussing the relationship between parental choice and school integration it is worth describing some of the more common conceptual errors and proposing a new conceptual framework that might be more appropriate. Once we agree on what we mean by integration and how to measure it, we can better discuss how it may be affected by school choice. In this chapter, I use the terms *integration* and *segregation* as simple opposites of each other.

## INTEGRATION . . . COMPARED TO WHAT?

A common error in popular discussion of school integration is to confuse a higher proportion of minority students with better integration. The most common manifestation of this conceptual error is found in arguments that private schools or schools of choice are less well integrated because they educate a lower percentage of minority students than do other schools. A more serious error, because it can be found more often in serious works of research, is the failure to establish a reasonable benchmark against which to compare the racial mixes observed in schools or school systems. By what standard can we say that one school or school system is better integrated than another school or school system?

I propose that, when possible, integration in schools should be compared against the racial composition of the broad community in which schools are located. For most schools the broad community is the metropolitan area. The comparison should not normally be limited to an attendance zone, school district, or city limits—as is the case in many studies of charter school segregation (See UCLA Charter School Study, 1998; Cobb & Glass, 1999)—because these political boundaries may themselves be a product of or encourage segregationist behavior. To the extent that schools reflect the racial composition of the broader community in which they are located, they are well integrated. To the extent that they deviate from the racial composition of the broader community, they are poorly integrated.

If we are comparing different school systems in the same community we should assess how well, on average, schools in each system individually approximate the racial composition of the broader community. A school system is better integrated than another system in the same community if individual schools in that system, on average, more closely resemble the racial profile of the broader community. Having presented an argument for appropriately measuring levels of integration, I will now discuss the ways in which researchers and advocates make faulty comparisons between choosers and nonchoosers.

## Don't Compare Choosers to Nonchoosers

A very common error in studies of the relationship between parental choice and integration is to compare the demographic characteristics of the families that participate in choice programs with the demographic characteristics of eligible families that do not participate. If choosers appear more advantaged (or are more likely to be White) than nonchoosers, then these studies conclude that choice exacerbates segregation. This approach is conceptually flawed for two reasons. First, integration is an outcome. We do not want to know whether choosers are different from nonchoosers; we want to know whether offering choices produces better results in terms of integration.

The fact that choosers differ from eligible nonchoosers does not tell us much about the relationship between choice and integration. It only tells us what we already knew: More-advantaged people are more likely to participate in a program than less-advantaged eligible people.

This observation could be made of virtually every government antipoverty program. The people who participate in programs to receive subsidies such as food stamps or the earned income tax credit tend to be somewhat more advantaged than the people who do not participate but are otherwise eligible. Those disadvantages are precisely what reduce participation. But all these programs may successfully target disadvantaged groups even if they do not always reach the most disadvantaged of the disadvantaged. To condemn programs for failing to reach the very disadvantaged while they successfully reach the moderately disadvantaged is to condemn antipoverty programs altogether.

A second conceptual flaw in research that compares the characteristics of choosers with those of non-choosers is that it tends to ignore the educational choices that occur in the absence of official school choice programs. This approach obfuscates the limited and skewed type of school choice already in existence. Wealthy people can decide to purchase housing in areas with desired schools or pay private school tuition in addition to the property taxes they already pay. People of more modest means have difficulty finding housing in areas with desired schools and also find it burdensome to pay even a small private school tuition in addition to the property taxes they already pay. The result is that there is currently a limited American school choice system that is based almost entirely on one's ability to pay for residential choices.

Any assessment of a choice program, then, has to be made in light of this already-existing wealth-based choice system. The question is whether expansion of choice produces better or worse integrated schools, yet, as I argue, many popular research studies compare choosers with nonchoosers and conclude that since the more advantaged are more likely to take advantage of school choice, choice leads to increased segregation (Heise & Nechyba, 1999; Henig, 1996; Wilms & Echols, 1993).

## Montgomery County

Henig's (1996) analysis of a public school choice program in Montgomery County, Maryland, is a widely cited study that suffers from these two conceptual flaws. Henig observes that "while many minorities participated, their rate of participation was not as great as that of whites" (p. 103). While this finding shows that participants may differ from nonparticipants, it does not address whether the program helps, hurts, or has no effect on integration.

In fact, in the case of Montgomery County it appears that having a higher rate of participation among White families probably contributed to having more integrated schools. The reason for this is that the schools that were selected to house the magnet school programs were located in minority neighborhoods and housed a disproportionate number of minority students. By encouraging more White students to seek transfers into these disproportionately minority schools, the public school choice program helped produce more integrated schools.

This is the case even though, as Henig observes, more White students tended to request transfers to participating schools with a higher proportion of Whites and more minority students tended to request transfers to schools with a higher proportion of minority students. If all transfer requests had been accepted, 8 of the 14 participating schools would have had a racial composition that more closely approximated the racial composition of the school-aged population in Montgomery County (where Whites are 66.67%), 5 schools would have a racial composition that was less representative of the county, and 1 school would have experienced no change. As Henig reports, school officials rejected certain requests for transfer to ensure that school integration was always improved, so the actual results were even more favorable to integration. But even if the officials had not rejected any requests for transfer, there would have been a net improvement in integration in Montgomery County public schools as a result of its public school choice program.

Observing a better result in terms of integration despite a disproportionately higher number of White participants and despite the observation that White and minority students tended to seek transfers to schools with a larger number of their own group shows the danger of examining integration by looking at the characteristics of choosers rather than by looking at results. The results were favorable to integration despite the observations about choosers because White students were selecting magnet programs in schools with disproportionately high minority populations. And even though minority students were more likely to be the majority of requested transfers to high-minority schools, there was a high enough proportion of White requests for transfers to those schools so that the resulting racial mix would have nevertheless been improved. Unless one looks at the results of choice on the racial mix in schools compared with a reasonable benchmark, one misses this positive effect of choice on integration.

While it is very common to find comparisons of the characteristics of participants and nonparticipants in the research on choice and integration, these comparisons are particularly unenlightening and potentially highly misleading.

## THE SCHOOLS ARE WELL INTEGRATED GIVEN THAT THEY ARE HORRIBLY SEGREGATED

Another common, and a more sophisticated, way of examining school integration is to measure how equally distributed racial and ethnic groups are within a school system. Measures such as the Index of Dissimilarity, the Index of Exposure, and the Gini Index are examples of this attempt to capture how integrated school systems are by measuring how evenly groups are distributed within that system. The difficulty with these approaches is that they take the racial composition of a school system as a given and then see how well distributed racial groups are given that overall racial composition. School districts or private school systems, however, might themselves be segregated. The shortcoming of these indices is that they do not compare the racial composition of schools against the broader community in which those schools are located.

It does not seem sensible to identify a school system as well integrated if it is racially homogenous compared with a reasonable benchmark but distributes that racial homogeneity evenly. For example, a school district that was 98% White would receive the highest possible score on the Index of Dissimilarity if every school within that district also had 98% Whites. This is not "integration" as we normally understand it. The school district may not be culpable for segregating students in the technical, legal sense. But this hypothetical district certainly cannot be described as integrated even though it has the highest possible score on the Index of Dissimilarity. This would especially be the case if the 98%-White school district were in the same metro area as an adjoining school district that was 98% minority.

The Index of Exposure measures the percentage of a racial group in the same school as the average member of another group. In the hypothetical district described above, the average White student is in school with 2% non-White students, producing a very low score on the Index of Exposure. But the average non-White student is in school with 98% White students, producing a very high score on the Index of Exposure. That is, the Index of Exposure would tell us that our hypothetical district was wonderfully integrated for non-Whites but horribly integrated for Whites. So is the school well integrated or poorly integrated? The Index of Exposure does not give us a straight answer, since the score depends on the group that is the focus of the analysis. There is also a "standardized" Index of Exposure that produces a single answer, but it does so by taking the racial composition of the district as a given, thereby introducing the same problems as are faced by the Index of Dissimilarity.

These approaches to measuring integration have been used by a number of researchers to assess the level of integration found in public and private schools. Coleman, Hoffer, and Kilgore (1982b) employed a measure similar to the Index of Exposure to determine whether public or private schools were better racially integrated. Their conclusion was that private schools were better integrated because the distribution of racial groups was more even there than in public schools. Similarly, in

1984 Robert Crain employed the Index of Exposure in a comparison of Catholic and public schools in Cleveland and Chicago and concluded that Catholic high schools were better racially integrated than their public school counterparts. Taeuber and James (1982) and Page and Keith (1981) responded that private schools should not be described as contributing to integration, because they have a lower percentage of minority students, on average, than do public schools. That is, they argued that private schools may have a more even distribution of minorities, but the general lack of minority students makes them relatively racially homogenous, not integrated.

A more even distribution of minority students in private schools does not demonstrate that those schools are better integrated. It is possible that private schools distribute students relatively evenly by race but have too few minority students to provide an integrated experience. The proper way to assess the level of integration in public and private schools is to compare the racial mix in the schools in each sector against the same reasonable benchmark. Analyzing the distribution of racial groups given the racial composition of a school system is interesting, but it does not really capture what we mean by integration.

## MEASURING INTEGRATION IN PUBLIC AND PRIVATE SCHOOLS

I have conducted a few studies comparing racial integration in public and private schools that I believe use appropriate definitions and measures of integration. To be sure, all these studies have their shortcomings, but they are nevertheless helpful in determining whether integration can be better produced when families are allowed greater choice in selecting schools.

In one study I analyzed the racial composition of a national sample of public and private school classrooms (Greene, 1998). In 1992 the authors of the National Education Longitudinal Study (NELS) surveyed a national sample of public and private school 12th graders. They also surveyed their teachers. The teacher survey asked the teachers how many total students they had in their class and how many minority students they had (*minority* was defined as Asian, Black, and Hispanic). From these questions I was able to calculate the percentage of minority students in the classrooms. More than half of public school students (54.5%) are in classrooms that are racially homogenous. That is, more than half of public school students are in classrooms that are more than 90% White or more than 90% minority. Fewer private school students, 41.1%, are in similarly segregated classrooms.

And private school students are more likely to be in classrooms whose racial composition is similar to the average racial composition in the nation, which, according to the responses in NELS, is 25.6% minority. More than a third (36.6%) of private school students are in classes whose racial composition is between 15% and 35% minority. Only 18.3% of public school students are in similarly integrated classrooms. When families choose, as they do when they select private schools, their children are in classrooms that are less likely to be racially homogeneous and are more likely to have a representative racial mix than when their children attend public schools.

This analysis of data from NELS is consistent with the appropriate framework for analyzing integration discussed above. It addresses how often classrooms in each sector are racially homogeneous and how often they are mixed in a way similar to the racial mix found in the nation. It would have been better if I had been able to compare the racial composition of each class against the racial composition in the broader community in which each class is located, but NELS does not provide that kind of data. The NELS data, however, do have the advantage of recording the racial composition of classrooms instead of school buildings. Given the frequency with which students are resegregated by tracking or course selection within school buildings, looking at the racial composition of classrooms is likely to be much more reliable than looking at the racial composition of school buildings (Chubb & Moe, 1996).

In another study, coauthored with Nicole Mellow, I observed a random sample of public and private school lunchrooms in Austin and San Antonio, Texas (Greene & Mellow, 1998). We recorded where students sat by race and then calculated how often public and private school students sat in racially mixed groups during lunch. A racially mixed group was one in which any of the five seats immediately adjacent to each student was occupied by at least one student who was of a different racial group. We found that 63.5% of private school students sit in a group where at least one student was of a different racial group, compared with 49.7% of public school students. If we make statistical adjustments for the city, the existence of seating restrictions, the size of the school, and the student grade level, the rate of private school students sitting in racially mixed groups increases to 78.9% and the rate for public school students drops to 42.5%. In the schools we observed, public school students are more likely to sit in racially homogeneous groups at lunch than are private school students.

This study of school lunchrooms is consistent with the standards for an appropriate study of integration discussed above. The study employed a reasonable definition of *integration*, the presence of racial heterogeneity (or the absence of racial homogeneity). This lunchroom study has the additional advantage of measuring integration (racial mixing) directly, so that it was not necessary or desirable to compare aggregate school compositions against the metropolitan area's racial composition. Normally we observe only the racial composition of schools as a whole and hope or assume that students have the positive experience of mixing with students of other backgrounds. In this study of lunchrooms we actually observe that positive social interaction directly. But this study does have its limitations. It reports observations from 38 schools in two cities. It is possible that these schools or these cities are somehow different from other sites in the country, limiting the confidence with which we can draw general conclusions about integration in public and private schools.

The analyses of data from NELS and this school lunchroom study are further limited by the fact that they involve private schools as they currently exist, not as they might be under a system of expanded school choice. It is possible that beneficiaries of school choice programs might behave in a way that produces less integration than what we see from people who currently choose private schools. Two studies of the effect of school choice programs on racial integration, however, suggest that this is not the case. Studies of the choice programs in both Cleveland and Milwaukee, the two long-running publicly funded voucher programs, show that voucher recipients attend better integrated schools than do their public school counterparts.

The Cleveland study found that nearly a fifth (19%) of voucher recipients attend private schools whose proportion of White students falls within 10% of the average proportion of White elementary students in metropolitan Cleveland (Greene, 1999). Only 5.2% of metropolitan Cleveland public school students are in similarly integrated schools. And more than three fifths (60.7%) of metro Cleveland public school students attend schools that are more than 90% White or more than 90% minority. Half of voucher recipients attend similarly segregated schools. A family moving for work in the Cleveland area would have better odds at finding an integrated school experience for their children if they enrolled in the choice program than if they were randomly assigned to a Cleveland area public school.

The study of the school choice program in Milwaukee conducted by H. Fuller and Mitchell (1999) has similar results. In 1998–99, they observed that 58% of Milwaukee public elementary students attended schools with more than 90% or fewer than 10% minority students. Only 38% of elementary school students in a large sample of Milwaukee Catholic schools were in similarly segregated schools. In 1998–1999, students enrolled in Catholic schools amounted to more than half of the students enrolled in the Milwaukee voucher program.

Both the Cleveland and Milwaukee studies are consistent with the standards for an appropriate analysis of racial integration. In the Cleveland study, the racial compositions in both public and private choice schools were compared against the racial composition of the broader community in which those schools are located. The private schools participating in the choice program were less likely to be racially homogeneous than the public schools in metro Cleveland. And those private schools more closely approximated the racial composition of metro Cleveland than did public schools.

In Milwaukee, Fuller and Mitchell only examined evidence of racial homogeneity in public and private schools, not how closely they approximated the racial composition of the broader community. Nevertheless, they found strikingly less racial homogeneity in private schools. And if they had included public schools from the entire metropolitan area, the extent of racial homogeneity in public schools would likely have been much higher than what they reported. Neither the Cleveland nor Milwaukee studies compare the demographic characteristics of participants with those of nonparticipants. Instead, they look at results: the racial composition of schools after people make choices. Both studies support the finding that when choice is expanded, students are more likely to enroll in well-integrated schools.

Reardon and Yun (2002, and Chapter 3 this volume), however, have recently produced an analysis of national public and private school data in which they claim to find that private schools tend to be more segregated than public schools. They use a variant of the Index of Exposure and conclude that Black-White segregation is more severe in private school but Latino-White segregation is more severe in public school. In a letter to the *Wall Street Journal*, Reardon provided more-straightforward results, writing that 59% of students in private schools attend racially homogenous schools compared with 43% of public school students.

Unfortunately, a number of research design flaws prevent these findings from being more persuasive. First, the study (Reardon & Yun, 2002) overrepresents private elementary schools. The analyses they conduct compare the segregation for all, combined, grade levels of public school students against the segregation for all grade levels of private school students, combined. The difficulty with doing this is that we know that private elementary schools educate a higher percentage of all students than do private high schools. According to figures that Reardon and Yun provide in their own report, private elementary schools educate 11% of all students, while private high schools educate 8% of all students. By combining all grades in their analyses Reardon and Yun are giving extra weight to private elementary schools.

This introduces a serious bias, because elementary schools—public or private—tend to be more segregated than high schools, since elementary schools tend to draw their students from smaller, more racially segregated, neighborhoods. Overweighting private elementary schools therefore makes the private sector appear more segregated, when in fact it may just be educating a younger population. The correct way to analyze this would be to compare students in the same grade level in the public and private sector or to make a statistical adjustment for the differences in grade levels between the two sectors.

The skewing of their sample by grade level helps explain Reardon and Yun's claims that segregation is greater in Catholic schools than in public schools and is less in secular private schools than in public or religious private schools. In fact, all that the authors are revealing is that Catholic schools are heavily concentrated in the elementary grades and that secular private schools are heavily concentrated in the high school grades, while public schools are distributed roughly proportionately across all grades. The more relevant question is whether elementary, middle, and high schools controlled by one type of institution differ in their level of segregation from schools of the same grade level controlled by other types of institutions. Reardon and Yun's analyses do not help us address this question.

Second, Reardon and Yun's study focuses on the racial composition of the public and private sectors by examining segregation at the school level. Yet we know that schools may resegregate students within a school building by means of practices such as tracking, electives, and housing magnet schools within neighborhood schools. All these practices are much more common in public schools than in private, making an examination of school-level racial statistics potentially misleading in favor of public schools. Unfortunately, a significant number of public schools that appear to be integrated when one looks at their aggregate racial composition lack any meaningful interaction between students of different races because those students are never enrolled in the same courses. Ideally, studies of segregation would examine classroom racial composition or other indicators of racial mixing within school buildings to gauge the true level of segregation, although obtaining such data is sometimes quite difficult.

In studies that I have done that do not suffer from these two biases—overweighting private elementary schools and looking at potentially misleading school level results—I find that private schools, in fact, tend to be less racially segregated than public schools. My analysis of data from NELS compares the level of segregation for 12th-grade students in the public and private sectors. My analysis also focuses on results at the classroom rather than school-building level.

Of course, it could be the case that these results for a national sample of 12th graders might not hold true if we compared public and private school students in other grades. In fact, a team of researchers at the University of Arkansas led by Gary Ritter (Ritter, Rush, & Rush, 2002) has analyzed the classroom racial segregation in a national sample of kindergarten students using conceptual models and methods similar to those I advocate. Contrary to my results, the researchers' findings are that public school kindergarten classrooms tend to be less racially segregated. Yet the group also finds that Catholic schools are about as well integrated as public schools, while other private schools are less well integrated.

Unfortunately, kindergarten may be a particularly bad grade to examine in trying to assess the racial segregation in public and private schools. Many communities in the United States do not offer full-day public school kindergarten. In fact, according to the Department of Education only 15 states require districts to offer full-day kindergarten. Those who want full-day kindergarten where it is not available must purchase it from a private school, and the people who are willing and able to do this are disproportionately wealthy and White. The result is that private schools educate 18% of the kindergarten population, while that sector's market share drops precipitously to 11% for elementary school. And this nonrepresentative swelling of private kindergarten rolls with White families that may switch to public school for first grade artificially makes private schools appear segregated (too White) while artificially making public schools appear less segregated (not so White).

It would be nice to have results similar to those that Ritter's team and I have produced for each grade—kindergarten though 12th grade—but Reardon and Yun do not help us with this problem. The fact that their sample is skewed by grade level and that they examine school-level results instead of interactions within schools prevent their study from being as useful as either Ritter's or my work. And given that Ritter's analysis of kindergarten segregation is highly unrepresentative of elementary and secondary public and private schools, the best national comparison of racial segregation in public and private schools appears to come from my analysis of NELS. The evidence from NELS suggests that private school classrooms are significantly less segregated than public school classrooms.

## EXPLANATIONS

While these studies of choice and integration do not tell us why expanding choice promotes integration, two explanations are consistent with the results. First, choice may promote integration by detaching where students go to school from where they live. Most public school students are assigned to schools based on where they live, and housing patterns tend to be strongly segregated by both race and class. We would therefore expect that public schools would tend to reproduce the racial and class segregation in housing.

Public school attendance zones and district boundaries not only reproduce racially segregated housing patterns; they probably also encourage segregation in housing. Unwilling to risk a loss of value in what is for most people their single largest, most highly leveraged asset, many families cautiously prefer to be on the "right side" of school district and attendance zone lines. And historically, attendance zones and district boundaries were intentionally drawn to separate racial and ethnic groups. The enormous impact of that segregation has not been fully eliminated.

Freely chosen private schools, however, are not constrained by housing patterns. Private schools can and typically do draw students from across neighborhood and public school boundaries. Obviously there are constraints of distance and transportation, but the distance between racial neighborhoods is usually far more of a psychological and political difference than a physical one. Families may be willing to cross these barriers because they are drawn to the private school for some common purpose. People from different neighborhoods may be drawn to the same private school because they share its educational philosophy or emphasis on quality. They may be drawn because of a shared interest in religious or cultural instruction. These various overarching goals help private schools transcend the racial segregation found in housing.

Of course, many urban public school districts have at least some schools whose composition is not determined by where students live. Those schools, however, are only a small portion of all schools in the United States. In addition, even if public schools draw students from outside their attendance zones they almost never draw students from across school district boundaries. In both Cleveland and Milwaukee public school districts, for example, there are or have been numerous magnet school, busing, and other programs where students attend schools outside of their attendance zones. But all these programs are seriously compromised in their ability to produce integrated schools by the fact that the school districts themselves are remarkably racially homogeneous. Students can be moved all around Cleveland or Milwaukee school districts, but they cannot easily be moved to integrated schools, because there are simply too few White students in the districts.

Private schools in central Cleveland and Milwaukee, however, do not face this constraint. Those private schools can attract students from all over their school district as well as from outside of the school districts to produce more racially heterogeneous schools. Being free from school district as well as attendance zone constraints is an important advantage for private schools in producing racially integrated schools.

Second, freely chosen private schools may promote integration because families are more likely to trust the operators of those schools to manage integration more successfully. Integration raises various concerns, some reasonable and some not, in some parents' minds, mostly concerning safety and discipline. Various surveys have shown that parents, students, teachers, and administrators report much higher confidence in the safety and discipline offered by private schools. In particular, there are reports of significantly fewer racial conflicts in private schools (despite the greater level of racial heterogeneity described above).

Parents are more willing to cross attendance zone and district boundaries to send their children to racially mixed schools when they have confidence that the integration will be managed successfully. This may further help explain why Cleveland and Milwaukee public schools have been unable to produce integrated schools, despite years of efforts at busing and magnet programs, while the voucher programs in both cities appear to be doing a better job of producing integrated schools. In Cleveland and Milwaukee many families have avoided integration in public schools that they do not trust by moving to suburban public schools. The private schools in those cities appear to be more successful at keeping families in the city and in integrated school settings because the families may simply trust those schools more.

## IMPLICATIONS

Once we have a proper definition and approach to measuring integration, we see that the evidence suggests that freely chosen private schools are more likely to be integrated than are public schools. This advantage of private schools in integration is probably caused by the fact that private schools do not determine their student composition based on racially segregated housing patterns and by the fact that parents appear to trust that private schools will manage integration better.

The implications of these findings and explanations for developing policy that is conducive to school integration are also clear. We are likely to get more integration if we adopt policies, such as private school choice, that allow people to select schools unconstrained by where they live or how much money they have. The inclusion of private and especially religiously affiliated schools in the range of school options that are available to people is particularly important because these are the schools that parents appear to trust more to manage integration successfully.

But how should these choice programs be regulated? It is not clear that any regulation is necessary or desirable for the purposes of promoting integration. One need only look at the higher level of integration that currently exists in largely unregulated private schools to see support for this position.

The school choice programs in Cleveland and Milwaukee impose more serious regulations than are normally placed on private schools. In both Cleveland and Milwaukee, participating private schools are prohibited from discriminating in their admissions. In Milwaukee, schools are also required to accept voucher students by lottery when seats are oversubscribed. In addition, participating private schools in Milwaukee are required to accept the voucher as payment in full for tuition. But in Cleveland, participating private schools are allowed to accept students according to their own policies (as long as they do not discriminate) and are allowed (in fact, required) to charge a nominal tuition copayment. Despite the more lax regulations in Cleveland vis-à-vis Milwaukee, the participating private schools in Cleveland show about as much advantage over the public schools in producing integration. The better integration appears largely to be a function of removing the constraints on choosing schools, not the imposition of regulations.

In fact, the expectation implicit in most of the chapters in this volume is that there must be regulations imposed on choice to make it consistent with integration. This reveals a predisposition toward failed approaches of the past. The assumption in these past efforts is that people will not voluntarily choose integrated schools and need to some extent to be forced to integrate. This is the assumption behind busing. It is also the assumption behind magnet programs in which choices are restricted (regulated) by required racial proportions or geographic boundaries.

Too often these efforts to force people to integrate result in people fleeing the political jurisdictions that attempt to force their behavior. Efforts at forcing integration also increase popular mistrust of the authorities in whom people must have confidence if they are going to attempt integration. And it is no small irony that the same government institutions that mandated segregation for much of the history of public education in this country are the same ones now mandating integration. One should not be surprised to find deep suspicion on the part of disadvantaged groups about the intentions of these authorities who previously required them to attend segregated schools.

Ultimately, we will only succeed in producing integrated schools when people are willing to send their children to integrated schools on a voluntary basic. That requires removing the financial and housing barriers to integrated schools and allowing families greater access to private, mostly religious, schools in which people have confidence with respect to integration. Some people may never voluntarily integrate. But these people have also escaped coerced integration by moving to racially homogeneous areas.

Rather than shaping policy around a relatively small, extreme population with which no approach is likely to be successful, we should concentrate on making policy that addresses the needs and concerns of the vast majority of families. Most families are primarily interested in finding a quality education for their children that will impart economically useful skills and socially appropriate behavior and values. Most parents do not mind if schools are also integrated as long as these other goals are addressed. That is, many parents are largely indifferent to integration as a goal in itself; and in that respect they probably have perspectives different from those of some researchers of school choice. But if parents unconstrained by housing are allowed to choose schools in which they have confidence, the net effect is likely to be a marked increase in school integration.

In attempting to promote integration, policymakers should imitate the first rule of doctors: Do no harm. Assigning students to schools based on where they live, attempting to force them to attend different schools that are integrated, and regulating their choices have done plenty of harm already.

# Chapter 3

# Private School Racial Enrollments and Segregation

JOHN T. YUN and SEAN F. REARDON

Historically, analyses of school segregation in America have focused almost exclusively on segregation within the public school sector. Where private schools are included in discussions of segregation, it has been to speak to concerns about how private schools affect public school segregation by selectively siphoning students from the public sector. In particular, private school racial enrollment patterns are often invoked in debates about school choice and voucher programs, as hypothetical outcomes with reference to specific changes that occurred in a very limited number of schools where choice programs were implemented (Coleman et al., 1982b; Green & Mellow, 1998; Levin, 1999; Taeuber & James, 1982).

These studies usually note that the proportion of minority students in public schools is higher than the proportion of minority students in private schools, implying that the private sector is more segregated than the public sector (Levin, 1999). However, differences in the racial composition of enrollments in the public and private sectors tell us only that there is segregation *between* the public and private sectors; they tell us nothing about the presence or extent of segregation *within* the private sector. To date, no large-scale study of the patterns of school segregation among private schools has been done. This chapter provides a description of racial segregation in the private school sector at a time when the possibility of private school choice is increasingly entering the public debate.

Given the current educational policy climate, in which private school choice and voucher programs are often presented as means of escape from largely segregated and failing public systems, we need a better understanding of these private school enrollment patterns. Florida, for example, under its Opportunity Scholarships Program has allowed students from failing public schools to receive vouchers to attend private schools in the state; after the 2001 *Zelman* ruling, several other states are considering similar legislation. While these changes are being debated in Congress and statehouses, a largely unanswered and unexamined question hangs over this controversy, namely, What does the private school system look like in these places? Are students leaving a highly segregated public system only to enter an equally segregated private one? Unless we believe that public money should be spent to send students to a segregated private school environment—a situation we have spent the better part of 50 years dealing with in the public sphere—the framing of school segregation as a public school problem must be broken. The first step in that process is to plot the current private school segregation landscape.

In addition, school segregation should not be measured solely between two racial groups—as it has been in the past—since the levels of racial diversity in the United States are increasing so rapidly. Instead, relationships between racial groups should be thought of multiracially. When we begin to think of segregation in multiracial terms we begin to see some of the complexities that are becoming the reality of the schools our children are attending. For instance, Black-White measures may incorrectly estimate how racially isolated a group would be, since Black and White students may be attending schools with substantial Latino or Asian populations. How these multiracial schools differ from our traditional picture of segregated schools is unclear, but without incorporating this perspective into examinations of school segregation these complexities are sure to be overlooked.

In this chapter we bring these two pieces—segregation in the private sector and the multiracial reality of our school system—together. We flesh out the current data regarding private school segregation by mapping the current state of private school segregation between Black, White, Latino, Native American, and Asian students nationally and in selected metropolitan areas around the United States. In order to accomplish this, we calculate multiple measures of private school segregation for the year 1998 using the Private School Survey (PSS) and the Common Core of Data (CCD) provided by National Center for Education Statistics. Specifically, we use the multiracial Theil's entropy index of segregation in conjunction with the exposure index. These measures will allow us to examine private school segregation by region, race, and levels of aggregation (metropolitan area, central city, and suburb) as well as by private school sector (Catholic, non-Catholic religious, and secular private).

Our goals are primarily descriptive, since very little research exists describing patterns of racial enrollment in private schools (Reardon & Yun, 2002). In particular, we address three questions in this chapter: (a) How much racial segregation and isolation is there within the private school sector? (b) How much of this segregation occurs within and between private school sectors (Catholic, other religious, nonsectarian)? (c) How do these patterns vary by region, race, and metropolitan area status (central city, suburban)?

## METHODS

Reardon, Yun, and Eitle (2000) have recently shown that, unlike other segregation indexes, Theil's entropy index of segregation can be used to break down the total segregation between multiple ethnic/racial groups into components that indicate what portion of the total segregation is caused by segregation between two or multiple groups. Theil's index will also allow us to decompose the total metropolitan area segregation into that between private school sector components, which will describe the amount of segregation caused by separation of the races between Catholic, secular, and non-Catholic private schools. Theil's index can further be decomposed to highlight differences in segregation between central city, and suburban private schools. Finally, in both its dichotomous and multiracial forms, the entropy index is highly correlated with more common measures of segregation, including the Index of Dissimilarity and the Gini Index (James & Taeuber, 1985; Massey & Denton, 1988; Reardon, 1998; Reardon & Firebaugh, 2002; Reardon & Yun, 2000). Because of this versatility, we will use Theil's entropy index to examine segregation among all racial groups, and the private school sectors. Theil's index can be described as measuring the diversity of a subunit (school) relative to the overall diversity of a larger area (metropolitan area, district, or nation), then taking the weighted average of that difference over the larger unit. $H$ ranges from a minimum of 0 when all subunits have diversity equal to the overall diversity (perfect desegregation) to a maximum of 1 when the diversity of each individual subunit is 0 (complete segregation) (For a further discussion about the properties and derivation of H, see Reardon & Firebaugh, 2002; Reardon, Yun, & Eitle, 2000). For our purposes, however, it is more important to observe the relative levels of segregation between the sectors than to know exactly what each individual value of *H* means.

While Theil's index has the advantage of being multiracial and decomposable, the exposure index (*P\**) has the advantage of being easily interpretable. The exposure index can be thought of as the percentage of a particular racial group in the school of the average student of another group (Orfield, Bachmeier, James, & Eitle, 1997; Orfield, Glass, Reardon, & Schley, 1993). In other words, an Asian-White exposure index of 59% could be interpreted as the percentage of White students in the school of the average Asian student. In this chapter, we calculate exposure indexes for Asian, Black, Latino, Native American, and White students to show how exposure differs by race, region, and sector. The ease of interpretation we find using *P\** connects well with the flexibility and complexity allowed by *H*.

Overall, our analysis will consist of two primary pieces, a national look that aggregates the data to the national level, and a local look that analyzes the patterns of segregation in selected metropolitan statistical areas (MSA). The national analysis will provide a general picture of segregation in the private school sector, while the local view will provide specific examples of how segregation is distributed in local contexts—for example, places where private school voucher programs are being contemplated or implemented.

The exposure index will be used to illustrate mostly national and regional trends between the public and private school sectors and within the private school sector. We will calculate a multiracial Theil's entropy index for both the national and local MSA analysis, then take advantage of Theil's properties to decompose it in various ways, which will clarify how the national and local multiracial private school segregation is distributed. Specifically, we will disaggregate the national and local segregation into between central city and suburb components, as well as within and between private school sector components. These calculations are very important, since they illustrate the many ways in which segregation can be distributed throughout a metropolitan area and may reveal many important relationships. For instance, if a high proportion of the private school segregation is found to be between the central city and suburbs, this will indicate that private school segregation, like public school segregation, may be largely attributable to housing patterns, since many more minorities live in central cities than the suburbs. Further, it indicates that although people can cross city/suburb boundaries to attend private schools in the suburbs, they tend not to. Such information could be very important in debates surrounding questions of school vouchers and choice.

## DATA

Our data come primarily from three sources: (a) the 1997–98 CCD (National Center for Education Statistics, 2000a); (b) the 1997–98 Private School Survey (PSS) (National Center for Education Statistics, 2000b); and (c) the October Current Population Surveys (CPS) from 1998, 1999, and 2000 (Bureau of the Census, 2000).

The CCD is a data set containing enrollment data—including racial/ethnic enrollments—for every public school in the United States. For the 1997–98 school year, every state except Idaho reported racial/ethnic enrollments in the CCD. The PSS is a similar data set for the universe of private schools in the 1997–98 school year. Both the CCD and PSS contain geographic identifiers that allow us to tabulate enrollment figures by public school district, metropolitan area, state, and region. The CCD and PSS do not, however, contain adequate family-income or poverty-status data to allow us to examine public and private school enrollment data by income. The October CPS provides counts of public and private school enrollments by race/ethnicity, family income, and geography (central city, suburb, rural). We use CPS data to examine private school enrollment rates by income and to provide detailed tabulations by urbanicity.

## RESULTS

### Private School Enrollment Patterns

The data in Table 3.1 indicate that the private school sector enrolls approximately 10% of all U.S. students, and this number has been very consistent across the years (Henig & Sugarman, 1999). Table 3.1 also shows the distribution of both public and private school students by region. The largest number of private school students are enrolled in the South (28.9%)—although roughly similar numbers of students are enrolled in both the Northeast and Midwest—and the fewest in the West (18.7%).

Another important factor is where schools are located by type of private school. For instance, in the private sector the greatest number of non-Catholic religious private schools is in the South and the fewest in

**Table 3.1.** Number and Percentage of Students Enrolled in Public and Private Schools by Region

| Region | Public | Private | Total | % Public Enrollment | % Private Enrollment |
|---|---|---|---|---|---|
| Northeast | 8,004,999 | 1,247,780 | 9,252,779 | 17.7 | 25.7 |
| Midwest | 10,547,462 | 1,296,885 | 11,844,347 | 23.3 | 26.7 |
| South | 16,200,001 | 1,406,572 | 17,606,573 | 35.9 | 28.9 |
| West | 10,419,879 | 911,621 | 11,331,500 | 23.1 | 18.7 |
| Total | 45,172,341 | 4,862,858 | 50,035,199 | 100.0 | 100.0 |

Source: Common Core of Data, 1997–1998; *Private School Survey*, 1997–1998

the Northeast. In addition, the most Catholic schools are in the Midwest and the fewest in the South, and secular private schools are located relatively uniformly in all regions except the Midwest, where the fewest secular schools are located. This information is important because it relates to the different nature of the private school segregation problem. Depending on the region, which schools would be most affected by private school vouchers or which schools contribute most to the region's segregation will change. In other words, it is important to recognize that the private school sector is not monolithic. Instead, it is composed of many different types of schools whose importance is related to such variables as region, and possibly suburban, central city, and rural location.

The distribution of schools is consistent with the change in the structure of private schools. In 1970, 70% of the private schools were Catholic; by 1997–98 fewer than 30% were Catholic, with 40% other religious (Henig & Sugarman, 1999) and 30% secular. The fastest growing sector in the past 30 years has been conservative Christian schools (Henig & Sugarman, 1999)—making up about 14% of private schools in 1997–98.

Table 3.2 shows the racial composition of public and private school enrollment in the United States and by region. These results confirm what many other authors have observed: White students are overrepresented in the private sector, and Black and Latino students are underrepresented. These differences in enrollment by race are a strong indication of segregation between the public and private school sectors. This pattern is most apparent in the South, where White students compose 58% of the public school population and almost 80% of the private school

**Table 3.2.** Public and Private School Racial Distribution by Region

| Public | White | Black | Hispanic | Asian | Native American | Total |
|---|---|---|---|---|---|---|
| Northeast | 68.9 | 15.3 | 11.5 | 4.0 | 0.3 | 100.0 |
| Midwest | 78.6 | 13.9 | 4.6 | 2.0 | 0.9 | 100.0 |
| South | 58.5 | 26.4 | 12.4 | 1.9 | 1.0 | 100.0 |
| West | 52.3 | 6.6 | 29.7 | 8.9 | 2.4 | 100.0 |
| *U.S. Totals* | *63.6* | *16.9* | *14.4* | *3.9* | *1.2* | *100.0* |
| **Private** | White | Black | Hispanic | Asian | Native American | Total |
| Northeast | 77.7 | 11.0 | 7.5 | 3.7 | 0.2 | 100.0 |
| Midwest | 85.4 | 8.2 | 3.9 | 2.0 | 0.4 | 100.0 |
| South | 79.8 | 9.9 | 7.4 | 2.7 | 0.3 | 100.0 |
| West | 64.7 | 6.4 | 15.1 | 12.7 | 1.2 | 100.0 |
| *U.S. Totals* | *77.9* | *9.0* | *7.9* | *4.6* | *0.5* | *100.0* |

*Source:* Common Core of Data, 1997–1998; *Private School Survey*, 1997–1998

population, and black students compose 26% of the public school population and only 10% of the private schools. By default these levels of overenrollment by White students also mean that Black, Latino, and Asian students have the opportunity to be exposed to higher numbers of White students, since, proportionally, there are more White students present in the private sector for interaction, a premise we will address later in the chapter.

Some have argued that this difference in private school enrollment is the result of differences in incomes between White and minority students. The racial and ethnic differences in private school attendance rates are related in part, but not wholly, to differences in average income levels between White and non-White families. White families' income levels are, on average, higher than those of Black and Latino families. According to the October CPS (CPS, 1998–2000), students from wealthier families are, not surprisingly, more likely to attend private than public schools. Only 3–5% of students from the lowest income families (those with annual incomes of less than $20,000) are enrolled in private schools, compared with 16% of those from families with annual incomes of above $50,000. Almost two thirds of students in private schools (63%) are from families with incomes greater than $50,000; less than 40% of students in public schools are from similar families. Likewise, only 8% of private school students are from families with incomes of below $20,000, compared with more than 22% of public school students.

Because the CPS does not include data on the schools attended by students, other than whether they are public or private, no school-level breakdowns are possible by income level. The PSS data set, which does include individual school information, does not, however, include any socioeconomic status information on students or their families; so again, no school-level breakdowns are possible by income level.

Despite the strong association of income and private school attendance rates, the income differences between White, Black, and Latino families do not explain racial/ethnic differences in private school attendance rates. Table 3.3 shows private school enrollment rates, by race/ethnicity and family income, in 1998–2000. At every income level, White students are more likely to be in private schools than are Black and Latino students. In the lower part of the income distribution—at income levels of below $30,000—Whites are roughly twice as likely to attend private schools than are Black and Latino students. The enrollment ratio

**Table 3.3.** K–12 Private School Enrollment Rates, by Race and Family Income, 1998–2000

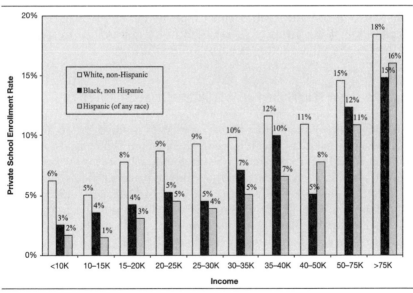

*Source:* Current Population Surveys, 1998–2000

narrows at the top of the income distribution, but White private enrollment rates are still two to four percentage points higher than Black and
Latino rates even among those families earning more than $50,000 annu-
ally.

The fact that white family incomes are, on average, greater than
those of Blacks and Latinos coupled with the fact that White private
school enrollment rates are higher, at all income levels, than those of
Blacks and Latinos means that middle- and upper-middle-class White
students are substantially overrepresented in private schools. In fact,
more than half (53%) of all private school students in 1998–2000 were
non-Latino White students from families with annual incomes of over
$50,000. The comparable figure in public schools was 32%.

A final interesting feature of private school enrollment is its distribution by metropolitan status—that is, whether the student attends
school in a central city, suburb, or rural area. Unlike public schools,
which enroll most of their students in the suburbs, private schools enroll
most of their students in the central city (Common Core of Data, 1997–
1998; Private School Survey, 1997–1998). This fact makes the racially
skewed private school enrollment even more interesting, since central
cities have a higher proportion of minority students than do the suburbs,
so one would expect private schools to have proportions of minority
students similar to, or greater than, those found in public schools. This
enrollment distribution also suggests that there is more demand for private schooling in the central cities than in the suburbs and that we
should look at the levels of segregation in these locations to see if they
are higher than those in the suburbs and by how much.


## PATTERNS OF PRIVATE SCHOOL SEGREGATION

In public and private sectors the most racially isolated group are White
students; however, in private schools the average White student is even
more isolated than in public schools. In public schools the average White
student attends a school that is 81% White; in private schools they attend
schools that are 88% White (Common Core of Data, 1997–1998; Private
School Survey, 1997–1998). Private school White students are in schools
with half as many Black students as public school White students, and
one third as many Latinos (Reardon & Yun, 2002).

Nationally, it appears that Black students face essentially the same
situation in private schools as in public schools, with similar exposure
to White students in both sectors: 32% in public schools and 34% in
private schools. The level of their isolation is very high, given that Black

students make up just 17% of the nation's enrollment, and the average Black student is in a school where approximately 54% of the students are Black. However, the similarity in these numbers hides the true level of segregation occurring in the private sector. It is important to note that the public sector is 64% White and the private sector 78% White. This difference (14%) in enrollment of white students for the private sector provides much more opportunity for White/minority interaction in the private sector. However, we find that the exposure rate is similar between sectors. This means that while private schools have more White students to distribute than do public schools, they do it even more poorly than do public schools. Thus, seeming numerical equality represents a greater inequality in distribution within the private school sector.

When compared with those in the public sector, Latino students in the private sector have greater exposure to White students and a slightly greater exposure to Asians, but less exposure to Black students. Asian students in private schools show similar differences when compared with their public school peers. Asian students show a greater number of White and Asian students in their schools, and fewer Latino and Black students. Asian students also show the highest exposure of students of all races—except Latino students themselves—to Latino students in both the private and public school sectors. This is most likely a regional story, as Asian and Latino students tend to live in the same areas of the country. So, in general, when there are differences in exposure by race, we are seeing private schools that have higher percentages of White and Asian students and fewer Black and Latino students when compared with their public school counterparts.

The national trends of public and private schools are not the entire story. As we discussed earlier, the private school sector is not monolithic and is made of several sectors that may have very different enrollment characteristics. Across the various private school types—Catholic, non-Catholic religious, and secular schools—the racial and social class differences of students between the sectors are instructive. White students in all three private sectors are more racially isolated than they are in public schools, with the average White student in non-Catholic private schools showing the highest level of isolation and Whites in secular private schools showing the lowest levels. The story for Black students is slightly more complicated. The levels of exposure of Black students to Whites and other Blacks in Catholic and non-Catholic religious schools are similar, at around 32% and 53%, respectively, but the exposure of Black students in secular schools is different from that of the other private schools, with the exposure to Whites higher, at 40.6%, and exposure to other Black students lower, at 47%. The story for Latino students is even more complex. The average Latino student in Catholic school is surrounded by the greatest percentage of Latinos, and has the smallest percentage of White and Black students with her in school. Secular schools show the highest percentage of Black students in the school of the average Latino student (14%) and 50.4% White students in the school of the average Latino.

Across the board, we see that secular schools show the highest percentage of exposure to Black students across all racial groups. This indicates that African American students are less racially isolated in secular schools when compared with those in the other private school sectors. Secular schools also show the highest level of exposure between Asian students and other races. Catholic schools show the highest percentage of Latino students for all racial groups. Non-Catholic religious schools show the highest level of racial isolation for White students (90.1%), and secular schools show the highest levels of White enrollment in the schools of all other races.

Another interesting way to break down the data is the aggregate central city–suburb story for Black and White students. Since only selected metropolitan areas have significant numbers of Asian, Latino, and Native American students, we will not discuss them in the aggregate, but their numbers are listed in Table 3.4. The percentage of Black students in the school of the average Black student in the central city is 60%; in the suburbs that same statistic is only 40%. Clearly, in the suburbs Black students are much less racially isolated than in central cities. In fact, all the races show more White students in schools in the suburbs and more minority students in the schools of all races. One could simply say that there are more White students in the suburbs so there *should* be more in suburban private schools; however, if this were simply the case one would expect a commensurate reduction in the percentage of White students in the school of the average White student in central cities. This is *not* the case: Schools in the central city show 86.6% White students in the school of the average White and suburbs show 88.6% of this same group in the suburbs. This suggests that there is a nonrandom sorting of White students in the central cities that concentrates them in the same schools.

A more complex view of the level of segregation and isolation experienced by students of different races emerges from these data. Using the exposure index, we find that there is no simple answer to the question, Is the private sector more segregated than the public sector? For White students the answer is clearly yes—the private sector is more segregated for the average White student across region, private school sector, and metropolitan status. However, for Black, Latino, and Asian students the

**Table 3.4.** Racial Composition of Central City and Suburban Private Schools Attended by the Average Student of Each Race

| **Central City** | Racial Composition of School Attended by Average | | | | |
|---|---|---|---|---|---|
| Percentage of Race in Each School | White Student | Black Student | Latino Student | Asian Student | Native American Student |
| % White | 86.6 | 27.7 | 36.1 | 47.3 | 52.3 |
| % Black | 4.7 | 60.0 | 10.9 | 7.4 | 8.8 |
| % Latino | 5.1 | 9.0 | 46.5 | 12.0 | 11.2 |
| % Asian | 3.4 | 3.1 | 6.1 | 32.9 | 6.3 |
| % Native American | 0.3 | 0.3 | 0.4 | 0.4 | 21.3 |
| *Total* | *100.0* | *100.0* | *100.0* | *100.0* | *100.0* |
| **Suburban Schools** | Racial Composition of School Attended by Average | | | | |
| Percentage of Race in Each School | White Student | Black Student | Latino Student | Asian Student | Native American Student |
| % White | 88.5 | 46.2 | 48.4 | 57.3 | 52.5 |
| % Black | 3.8 | 40.3 | 8.4 | 6.6 | 6.8 |
| % Latino | 4.0 | 8.4 | 34.5 | 11.5 | 8.1 |
| % Asian | 3.4 | 4.7 | 8.2 | 24.1 | 5.7 |
| % Native American | 0.2 | 0.4 | 0.4 | 0.4 | 26.8 |
| *Total* | *100.0* | *100.0* | *100.0* | *100.0* | *100.0* |

*Source:* Common Core of Data, 1997–1998; *Private School Survey*, 1997–1998

question is more complex. With higher enrollments of White students in the private sector, the answer for Black students is the same: The private sector is more segregated than the public sector. For Latino and Asian students, the sectors appear equivalent or slightly more desegregated in the private sector.

## SEGREGATION IN THE PRIVATE AND PUBLIC SECTORS

The exposure index tells us a story about segregation in the private sector and between public and private schools across the different races.

What the exposure index gains in interpretability it loses by requiring many values to adequately describe multiracial relationships. Theil has the advantage of collapsing the relationship between multiple races into a single number that can be thought of as how much less diverse, on average, the schools are than their district as a whole. Although we do not show the formula for $H$ here, note that the within–central city component depends not only on the within–central city value of $H$, but also on the relative size and relative diversity of the central city. Segregation in places with large and diverse student populations contributes more to the within–central city segregation component than does comparable segregation in central cities that are small, homogeneous, or both (Reardon, Yun, & Eitle, 2000). The remaining portion of the total segregation cannot be reduced without some suburban–central city student transfers. We will now consider Thiel's index in relation to segregation in Chicago, Miami, and New York City.

### Segregation in Selected Metropolitan Areas

Most of the segregation we find is attributable to racial/ethnic isolation within the public sector, because the population of students in the public school sector is so much larger than that in the private school sector. It is also the case that the level of diversity in the public school sector is much larger than the diversity in private school sector. Both these factors contribute to a larger share of the segregation being attributed to the public school sector. However, by using selected metropolitan areas we can make the story a little bit more complex. (All data in this section come from the CCD, 1997–1998 and PSS, 1997–1998.)

As we saw earlier, the diversity of the school varies with its geographic location (either in the central city or suburbs). Thus, in our metropolitan-areas analysis we differentiate between central city and suburban schools to determine how private school segregation is distributed within and between private school sectors, and within and between the central city and suburbs.

We chose Chicago, Miami, and New York for specific reasons. All three are among the largest cities in the country and have very different populations. Chicago is one of the most segregated metropolitan areas in the nation and is predominantly Black and White. New York's metropolitan area is very diverse and currently has a privately funded private school voucher program up and running. Miami is also extremely diverse, and with the Florida voucher program also has the possibility of a voucher program distributing public school students into the private sector.

In Chicago, the total segregation in the public and private school sectors is the same. The total central city segregation is higher than the suburban segregation. We also see the same trends we saw in previous analysis: In the suburbs, non-Catholic religious schools have the highest level of segregation, while Catholic schools have the lowest level of segregation. Within the suburbs and central city there is very little segregation between the sectors, but segregation between the central city and the suburbs makes up 12% of the private school segregation.

The school segregation in the New York metropolitan area is very different from that in Chicago. First, the private school segregation is much higher than the public school segregation. Second, segregation in the non-Catholic private school sector is pronounced across city and suburbs. These values are extreme, especially when compared with the Catholic school and secular school segregation levels, particularly in the suburbs, where secular school segregation is a miniscule 0.08% and Catholic school segregation is 0.28%. Third, we find segregation between central city and suburban areas to be much lower than it was in Chicago and constituting only 2% of the total private sector segregation. Next, we hypothesize that even if all the segregation within the private school sectors in the central city were eliminated, there would still be a substantial amount of segregation left between these sectors—approximately 16%. Finally, in the central city all the private school sectors have higher levels of segregation than do the public schools; in this case, students in central city areas who leave the public sector will be entering a much more segregated environment, particularly if they entered the non-Catholic religious sector. More important, depending on the choices they make and the schools they decide to attend, their distribution may make the sector they enter even more segregated.

The segregation profile for the Miami-Hialeah metropolitan area is different from those of both Chicago and New York. Here—as in the New York area—the public school segregation is lower than the private school segregation. We also find the segregation in the secular private school sector to be the lowest when compared with that in the other private schools. In Miami, the Catholic and non-Catholic religious schools have very similar levels of segregation in both the central cities and the suburbs. However, non-Catholic religious schools contribute the greater share to private school segregation, with a combined 41.4% of the total. In addition, the combined between–private sector segregation contributes 12.7% to the total private school segregation as well. This is a much higher share than the between-sector segregation in Chicago, and lower than that in New York. Again overall, students leaving the public sector would be entering a more segregated private sector. The differences across Chicago, New York, and Miami reveal the importance of geographical context.


## DISCUSSION

In general, we have found that secular schools have lower levels of segregation for all racial groups and in both central cities and suburbs. We also have established that non-Catholic religious schools are associated with higher levels of segregation when compared with the other private school sectors. It is also generally true that central cities have higher levels of segregation than do the suburbs.

The exposure analysis yielded several other important findings. First, it is clear that deciding what *segregation* means in a multiracial world is no longer so simple. Sectors and regions are more or less segregated depending on which races and schools are examined. For example, White students are much more segregated in private schools than in the public sector and they are more segregated than any other group. However, when you move to Latino students and their exposure to other races in the secular private school sector we see they are in a less isolated position with regard to White and Asian students but are exposed to fewer Black students. The questions remain: Does that mean that this is a less segregated environment? Do more white and Asian students trade off against fewer Black students? The answers are not obvious. Two unequivocal findings are that White students are the most segregated in all sectors and across central city and suburban lines, and that for Black students, white students are distributed much more poorly in the private than in the public sector.

The most important finding from the analysis of *H* is that the profile of private school segregation can be extremely different depending on the specific metropolitan area. Despite the complexity, we do possess the analytical tools to examine these profiles and to assess the relative segregation within and between the school sectors.

### Educational Significance and Future Studies

In this era of school choice and private school voucher movements, we can no longer construct the problem of school segregation as only for the public sector. Critical questions of whether public money should be spent to subsidize the movement of children into a sector that can be highly segregated cannot be broached without knowledge of the segregation status of that sector. This approach has given us an important first step into the ecology of our schools, cities, and suburbs with respect to racial separation.

Our analyses of segregation patterns yield several important findings. First, private schools are more highly segregated than has been generally assumed, in some areas more segregated than public schools. In general, we have found that Catholic and other religious schools are the most segregated schools in the private sector, while secular private schools are the least segregated. It is also generally true that private school segregation is greatest in large urban areas with large Black populations and where residential segregation is substantial.

Another important finding is that Black-White segregation patterns do not correspond with Latino-White segregation patterns—a variety of regional, religious, and income factors affect Black and Latino patterns differently, resulting in distinct patterns of segregation. For instance, Black students face more segregation in the private sector, particularly among Catholic and other religious schools, than in the public sector. Latino students, however, are roughly equally segregated among public and Catholic schools, but less segregated in other religious and secular schools.

The assumption that minority students experience higher levels of integration with Whites in the private sector when compared with the public sector is simply not true, particularly for Black students and, to a lesser degree, Latino students. The discussion about the desirability of private schools has often included claims that minority students would get the same access to schools as do Whites if only the former had greater access to the private sector. In fact, Black students in the private sector are just as segregated from Whites as in the public sector. In addition, White students in the private sector generally attend overwhelmingly White schools, leading to extremely high levels of White racial isolation. Latino private school students make up a small fraction of private school enrollments, but they still experience schools that typically have substantial non-White majorities. Since private schools typically provide no free transportation for students, an increase in the minority percentages in these schools would be likely to increase segregation.

Important questions remain for researchers of school choice and student diversity. First, we only know *what* the segregation looks like in these areas; we don't know *why* it looks that way. We also need to have measures of socioeconomic class in the private school sector to see if the type of segregation we see in the private schools, is similar to that in the public schools where high levels of racial isolation and segregation are correlated with high levels of poverty (Orfield et al., 1993; Orfield & Yun, 1999). Overall, these findings present a picture of private school segregation that is varied and complex and that suggests that private schools, as now composed, are not a significant answer to the intensifying racial isolation in public schools and the increasing diversity of the school-age population. Policymakers, parents, advocates, and educators must consider the nature of private school segregation in order to develop policies that will best serve the needs our changing student populations.

## NOTE

We thank Stephen Matthews, Steve Graham, and Mike Stout for their help in preparing the data for this chapter.

# Chapter 4

# Where School Desegregation and School Choice Policies Collide

*Voluntary Transfer Plans and Controlled Choice*

AMY STUART WELLS and ROBERT L. CRAIN

Since the earliest efforts to dismantle racially segregated public school systems, parental-choice programs have had a tenuous relationship with school desegregation policies. In the years following the *Brown* decision, deregulated, freedom-of-choice programs were put in place throughout the South explicitly to thwart the possibility that large numbers of Black and White children would end up in the same schools (see Orfield & Eaton, 1996). Indeed, not until the 1970s did judges order more comprehensive desegregation remedies that included mandatory reassignment of Black and White students to the same schools (Yudof, Kirp, & Levin, 1992). But the judicial emphasis on mandatory plans was short-lived. By the early 1980s, the Reagan administration and other conservative groups began to lobby vigorously for choice-oriented, or "voluntary," desegregation plans designed specifically to ensure that White students were not subjected to mandatory reassignment, which they labeled "forced busing" (Mirga, 1982).

Still, the hundreds of voluntary desegregation plans that were established in the 1980s and 90s were more effective than the freedom-of-choice plans of the earlier era. In fact, many were created under court orders; thus, they were voluntary only from the parents' and students' perspectives and not from that of the school districts. Paradoxically, these voluntary desegregation orders are currently under attack by the same conservative groups that helped create them nearly 20 years ago, and federal court judges are obliging them in many cases (Savage, 2000). Indeed, with the current policy emphasis on non-desegregation-based school choice policies, such as charter schools and vouchers, advocates of school desegregation are losing political and legal ground in their fight for even the most benign of voluntary, choice-oriented school desegregation plans.

In this chapter we look closely at what we currently know about these voluntary desegregation programs and ask what we might learn from these policies that can inform current debates on school choice and racial diversity. We begin with the political context of these programs, which has shaped the way in which they have been portrayed—first as the very necessary alternative to mandatory assignment programs and, more recently, as an unnecessary race-based policy in the era of complete deregulation. We then review relevant literature on two popular forms of voluntary school desegregation, namely voluntary transfer programs—also called majority-to-minority transfer plans—and controlled choice programs. Many of the arguments made for and against "voluntary" school desegregation apply to magnet schools as well as voluntary transfer plans and controlled choice plans (see, for instance, Rossell, 1990).

Despite their political context, many of these choice-oriented school desegregation programs represent attempts by school districts, judges, and advocates to strike a delicate balance between individual parents' demands for choice and the broader, societal goal of equal opportunities for all. If for no other reason than to understand this balance, we should pay close attention to what these programs accomplished, how they accomplished it, and whose interests were served.

## THE "VOLUNTARY" VERSUS "MANDATORY" DESEGREGATION DEBATE

The parental choice programs known as freedom-of-choice plans accomplished little desegregation in the years following the *Brown* decision. In fact, few racially mixed schools existed until the Supreme Court ruled in a Virginia case, *Green v. New Kent Country School Board*, that formerly segregated school systems had an affirmative duty to eliminate racial discrimination "root and branch." The test of a school district's desegregation plan was its success in producing mixed-race schools (see Hendrie, 1999a; Yudof et al., 1992; and Wells, 1993).

In 1971, the Supreme Court took an even more directive stance, in *Swann v. Charlotte-Mecklenburg Board of Education*, when it stated that the courts could require school districts to use racial quotas, newly drawn attendance zones and transportation (or "busing") to correct racial segregation. These two Supreme Court rulings led to the creation of hundreds of mandatory reassignment plans, especially in the South. Indeed, during the Johnson and Nixon administrations, court-ordered school desegregation reassigned large numbers of southern White and Black students, along with a much smaller number of northern students, to desegregated schools—often against their parents' wishes (see Orfield, 1978; Wells, 1993; and Yudof et al., 1992).

Opponents of mandatory busing often blamed White flight on the 1970s' school desegregation policies as opposed to the myriad of other factors that also contributed to Whites' exodus from cities without school desegregation policies (see Orfield, 1978). In fact, there is ample evidence that White flight occurred in cities with no mandatory reassignment plans. For instance, the St. Louis Public Schools lost tens of thousands of White students (from 78% of the student population to 37%) between 1942 and 1967, well before any forced busing of students was even seriously considered (Wells & Crain, 1997). Other cities that experienced massive White flight with no mandatory reassignment desegregation plan in place include Atlanta and Chicago (Orfield & Ashkinaze, 1991).

Furthermore, research demonstrates that within areas affected by school desegregation plans, housing segregation decreases as families seek integrated neighborhoods so that their children can attend integrated *neighborhood* schools instead of being transported elsewhere (Farley & Frey, 1994). This is especially true in the South, with its large, countywide school districts, where the suburbs were often involved in desegregation. This occurred, Pearce (1981) argues, because there was less pressure in White suburbs to keep minorities out and Blacks became more interested in moving to the suburbs once their children were traveling to suburban schools. Still, school desegregation plans within a single urban district that is surrounded by separate suburban districts can lead to increased White flight across district boundaries, thus increasing housing segregation at the metropolitan level (Pearce, Crain, Farley, & Taeuber, 1984). This decline in White enrollments in urban school districts gave opponents of mandatory desegregation plans the evidence they needed to lobby against those programs.

Yet it was not simply the issue of White flight that fueled opposition to mandatory plans. Opposition was also grounded in the age-old arguments of "state rights" and "local control"—thinly veiled resistance to racial mixing and fierce anger at a government that forced it (see, for instance, Edsall, 1991; Orfield, 1969). Many Whites were outraged by court orders that reassigned students, particularly White students, to schools outside their neighborhoods, seeing these actions as the erosion of parents' and students' individual rights (Edsall, 1991).

By the early 1980s, opponents of forced busing found an important political ally in the Reagan administration, particularly the Justice Department, where the goal of dismantling mandatory reassignment plans became a mantra. In a 1984 address, then assistant attorney general for the Civil Rights Division of the Justice Department, William Bradford Reynolds (1984), argued:

> Our focus has turned from forced transportation and concentrated instead on desegregating dual school systems through an emphasis on voluntary student transfer techniques, open enrollment, neighborhood schools with neutrally drawn zones, and expanded educational opportunities designed to attract students to the public school, not to drive them away. (p. 10)

The political and judicial tide was quickly turning away from mandatory desegregation programs. Rossell and Glenn (1988) wrote that when faced with the possibility of a mandatory student assignment desegregation plan, school systems nationwide were quick to develop voluntary desegregation plans.

A new era of school desegregation had begun—an era that would offer yet another balance between the rights of individual parents to choose schools for their children and the rights of groups of children, particularly African American children, to gain access to higher-status schools and better educational opportunities. The reality of what these newer desegregation policies looked like and whom they benefited varied greatly across local contexts as advocates of racial integration squared off with proponents for greater parental choice. In the following sections we focus on two programs that fit under the umbrella term of "voluntary school desegregation plans": voluntary student transfer programs and controlled choice.

## Voluntary Student Transfer Programs—Desegregation by Choice

Voluntary transfer programs, whether they were created via a court order or implemented independently by school districts, generally operate under a majority-to-minority guideline. In other words, these programs are designed to allow students enrolled in schools in which their racial/ethnic group is the majority to transfer to schools in which their racial/ethnic group is the minority. This characteristic distinguishes these desegregation programs from more recent "open enrollment" policies of the 1990s that offer parents and students within- and cross-district school choice, but with no desegregation guidelines or goals (see Wells, 1993).

But the majority-to-minority component is where the commonality ends across voluntary transfer programs. For instance, some allow students school choices only *within* the boundaries of one, generally urban, school district. Cities that have in the past or currently operate such *intradistrict* transfer programs include Austin, Chicago, Los Angeles, and Houston.

More comprehensive transfer programs offer *interdistrict* choices through which students from urban school districts are able to attend suburban schools, and sometimes, suburban students can attend urban school districts. Metropolitan areas that house (or once housed) interdistrict programs include, Boston, Hartford, Milwaukee, St. Louis, and Portland.

Some transfer programs are part of larger desegregation remedies that can also include mandatory reassignments and magnet schools. Thus, some are more regulated than others—they include fairly strict racial guidelines about how many students of different racial/ethnic groups may transfer where and which schools must accept which students. Other programs are more deregulated in terms of racial guidelines and control over which schools participate and to what extent. Furthermore, some of these programs provide the transferring students and their families with information about their choices, free transportation and counseling and support services. Other programs place much more burden on the families to learn about their options and take advantage of them.

Given these differences, it is very difficult to draw general conclusions about the success or failure of these programs, especially in terms of their impact on racial diversity in and across public schools. Thus, we focus on three interdistrict, or city-to-suburban, transfer programs in Boston, Hartford, and St. Louis.

### City-to-Suburban Interdistrict Student Transfer Programs

Three of the best-known and most studied city-to-suburb plans are METCO in Boston, Project Concern in Hartford, and the St. Louis interdistrict transfer plan. There are important distinctions and similarities across these three programs. All three allow African American students (and Latino students, in some instances) from the cities to attend predominantly White suburban schools free of charge and with free transportation. Neither METCO nor Project Concern is court ordered, while the St. Louis program was created via federal court order. Also, St. Louis is a much larger and more comprehensive school desegregation program that included extra resources for urban school improvement and magnet schools. Ironically enough, both METCO and Project Concern were established in the 1960s, well before the Reagan era and the political support for voluntary school desegregation that came with it. The St. Louis plan, however, was started in the early 1980s, right in line with the shift toward more voluntary school desegregation.

Below, we provide a brief description of each of these programs, followed by a discussion of the research findings from these sites.

*Boston's METCO Program.* This interdistrict voluntary transfer program, which began in 1966, allows Black students from the city of Boston to attend schools in one of 16 different suburbs. METCO—an acronym for Metropolitan Council for Educational Opportunity—was founded by Black parents and activists who "originally saw the new program as a partial and temporary remedy for the poor conditions in Boston's then-segregated, predominantly black schools" (Eaton, 1999, p. 3). It preceded Boston's court-ordered and somewhat infamous school desegregation plan of the 1970s and 1980s.

During the first year of the METCO program, 220 Black students in the 1st through 11th grades traveled to schools in seven suburbs. In 1999, about 3,100 Boston students traveled to 37 participating METCO communities. About 4,300 men and women have graduated from the program in the past 3 decades (Eaton, 1999). Meanwhile, the waiting list of students who wanted to participate in the program was nearly 13,000 in 1999 (Eaton, 1999). By the mid-1990s parents were signing up to participate when their children were only a year old (Orfield et al., 1997). Furthermore, Eaton (1999) noted that although there are no admission standards for the program, "some districts employ informal standards for students to remain in their district and will 'counsel' students out because of discipline of other problems" (p. 6).

The state has funded most of the cost of the program—about $12.4 million per year. It operates through a central office in Roxbury, whose staff counsels and advises parents and students interested in the program, directs the student placements and transportation, and coordinates special programs such as college tours. In the suburban school districts, METCO personnel work with METCO students, parents, and educators in the suburban schools, often acting as advocates for the students and coordinators of the logistics (Eaton, 1999).

*Hartford's Project Concern.* Interdistrict school desegregation in Hartford began in 1966 with a voluntary urban-suburban student transfer program known as Project Concern. This program, financed by the National Institute of Education using Title I funds, randomly selected first- and second-grade Black students from four inner-city Hartford elementary schools to attend 60 predominantly White schools in 13 suburban school districts. By the 1990s, however, the program was funded in part by the state and in part by the participating school districts, which resulted in budget cuts and a reduction in the number of students who could participate. Thus, enrollment in the program was down to 680 students in 1993 from a peak enrollment of about 1,500 students in the late 1970s (see Piliawsky, 1998). Yet with the advent of a new school desegregation case remedy in 1997, Project Concern was expanded slightly to include 100 additional Hartford students (Piliawsky, 1998).

Project Concern has an interesting and rather paradoxical relationship with the recent school desegregation case in Hartford, filed in 1989. On the one hand, plaintiffs cited Project Concern as evidence that more desegregation would help improve the educational opportunities of African American students. On the other hand, the State of Connecticut argued that the existence of Project Concern since the 1960s was evidence that there had been good-faith efforts to desegregate the schools.

In 1996, when the state Supreme Court ruled in favor of the plaintiffs, it did not order any specific remedies, but instead directed the state's General Assembly and the executive branch to search for "appropriate remedial measures." By placing the responsibility for the remedy in the hands of the state legislature and the governor's office, the court set the scene for several years of political maneuvering. Finally, in the fall of 1998, several phases of a $3 million voluntary desegregation program were implemented, including the small expansion of the Project Concern program (Weizel, 1998).

*St. Louis's Inter-district Voluntary Transfer Plan.* The most visible component of a comprehensive desegregation 1983 court order in St. Louis was the voluntary interdistrict transfer plan offering Black students from the city the opportunity to transfer to 122 schools in the 16 suburban districts where Black students were less than 25% of their total student population at the time the agreement was made. Under the terms of the settlement, the 16 suburban districts were required to increase their Black student enrollments to at least 15%, but no more than 25% (see Wells & Crain, 1997).

The final court order emphasized student and parental choice instead of politically unpopular mandatory busing practices. The plan extended far beyond the faltering urban school system to include the wealthy, prestigious suburban schools. White suburban students, meanwhile, stay in their neighborhood schools unless they choose to transfer to a City magnet school. Black students who live in the city can choose to stay in their neighborhood school, enroll in a magnet schools, or transfer to a suburban school, provided there is space and the student does not have a poor disciplinary record. Suburban districts cannot deny African American students from the city admission because of grades or test scores (Wells & Crain, 1997).

The State of Missouri was ordered by the district court to pay the suburban school districts an "incentive payment," equivalent to their per-pupil cost, for each Black student who transfers to their schools. The state was also ordered to pay for the transportation system that allows Black students from the city to choose any suburban school. The state provides each of the 12,700 city-to-county and the 1,500 county-to-city "transfer students" one free round-trip ride from home to school each day. This round trip includes drop-offs or pick-ups for students attending before- or after-school programs. Also, because under the original plan Black students who lived anywhere in the city of St. Louis could theoretically transfer to any participating suburban school, provided there was room in that school, the cost of the transportation was high and the logistics of the daily commutes were complicated. During the peak years of the program in the early 1990s, the state contracted with bus companies for 700 buses and 125 taxicabs traveling nearly 10 million miles. The state was spending about $1,700 per student on transportation. The annual state cost for the program was close to $150 million by the mid-1990s.

In 1999, a new settlement agreement was reached in the St. Louis case that continues the urban-suburban transfer program without the court order for at least 10 more years (Pierce, 1999). After that, the Missouri state legislature will decide the fate of the program. Transportation will still be provided for transfer students, although the range of choices will be limited by a new zone system that matches individual suburban school districts with particular areas of the city. As of fall 1999, new city-to-suburban transfers who live in the zone for a certain suburban school district can only enroll in that district. In the first year of this revised settlement agreement, the number of students transferring into suburban schools from the city and vice versa remained steady (Pierce, 1999).

## RESEARCH EVIDENCE ON INTERDISTRICT VOLUNTARY TRANSFER PROGRAMS

When we look at the research literature, we see that all three programs have reduced racial segregation, at least for a limited number of students, in these three metropolitan areas (Eaton, 1999; Orfield et al., 1997, 1998; Wells & Crain, 1997). Still, none of them serves even close to a majority of the African American students in the three cities. Yet these plans may serve a larger number of students than any alternative plan could. Hartford and St. Louis both have segregated central cities, and both send a significant number of African American students to the suburbs. Hartford now sends close to 1,000 of its approximately 14,000 Black students—or 7%—to predominantly all-White suburban schools. Meanwhile, about 13,000, or 25%, of the Black students from the St. Louis public schools attend suburban schools through the voluntary desegregation plan. Boston's METCO program serves 3,100 Black students, or slightly less than 10% of all Black students in the Boston public schools.

The impact of these programs on the racial makeup of the predominantly White suburban school districts that receive the transfer students varies tremendously across and within these metropolitan areas. This impact is more substantial in St. Louis. Indeed, the nine St. Louis suburban school districts that had had 1983 enrollments that were 5% or less Black enrolled between 13 and 24% Black students by 1995 (see Wells & Crain, 1997). In Boston and Hartford, where the suburban school districts have much more control over which transferring students they accept, the impact has been less substantial, with some districts enrolling fewer than 100 transfer students in the entire district.

Despite some success, then, all three of these programs leave large numbers of students "behind" in urban public schools. Impediments to choice remain. In both Boston and St. Louis, parents have to learn about the program and how to sign their children up for it on their own. Thus, there is concern that only the most involved, connected, and efficacious parents will opt out of the regular urban public schools, leaving behind those parents who are not able to play as large a role in their children's schools.

For instance, in Boston, Orfield and colleagues (1997) found that about 17% of the students who participate in the METCO program come from families with household incomes greater than $50,000. Furthermore, about 36% of the METCO parents were college graduates, and 12% had graduate or professional degrees. All but 4% were high school graduates (Orfield et al., 1997).

According to suburban educators in St. Louis, some of this has occurred within the interdistrict transfer plan, although there is also evidence that those are the very students who do not last long in the suburbs (see Wells & Crain, 1997). An analysis of student test-score data demonstrates that the students going out to the suburban schools in St. Louis do have, on average, slightly higher test scores than the students who remain in the neighborhood schools in the city, but slightly lower test scores than the students who enroll in magnet schools in the city (see Lissitz, 1993, 1994; Wells & Crain, 1997). Hartford's Project Concern minimizes these issues by using a random lottery to accept students into the program.

These student selection issues across the three interdistrict plans also affect the research on each of these programs (Crain, Miller, Hawes, & Peichert, 1992). In Boston and St. Louis, no such experimental design can be used, because the transfer students are not chosen by lotteries. Still, despite these methodological differences, several of the findings about the effects of these programs on the lives of the transferring students are similar across the three metro areas.

First, research across these programs indicates that city-to-suburb transfer students were more likely to graduate from high school, go on to college, and ultimately work in higher-paying jobs than their city counterparts (Crain et al., 1992; Easton, 1999; Wells & Crain, 1997). Part of their success in higher education and the labor market was attributed to their being more comfortable around Whites and feeling that they were more accepted in predominantly White situations (Braddock, 1980).

Another consistent finding is that students felt more comfortable about themselves and their aspirations for social advancement (Lissitz, 1993, 1994). Moreover, through exposure to college application procedures, students understood the steps they needed to take to realize their aspirations and move into previously unfamiliar institutions. In turn, these desegregation experiences helped to enable blacks to live in integrated neighborhoods and hold jobs traditionally closed to them (Crain et al., 1992).

Finally, students developed the ability to transcend structural barriers, to understand the relationship between race and class, and to feel confident about their abilities to compete in integrated environments. Like the findings from the Project Concern graduates, the METCO graduates said that their suburban experience influenced their "personal attitudes, opinions and actions" leaving them more "comfortable" in predominantly White settings and more willing to enter such settings than they think they would have been if they had not gone to suburbia. Furthermore, those who work in predominantly White settings were often asked to play a leadership role in improving race relations and increasing diversity within the workplace. Another form of bridging includes challenging racial stereotypes and discrimination and trying to make racial exchanges into enriching rather than threatening experiences.

African American city students also knew that going to school with white middle- and upper-class students had a lot of added advantages (Zweigenhaft & Domhoff, 1991). For instance, the White suburban schools in St. Louis—unlike the urban schools serving poor and Black students—are focused on preparing students for college and white-collar lives. Thus, they are intricately linked, through a complex network, to the admissions offices of the top universities (Wells & Crain, 1997).

These different urban-suburban school cultures and institutional expectations may help explain why the longitudinal studies of African American student achievement rates in county versus city schools has found consistently that the transfer students who participate in the interdistrict school desegregation program show a "consistent, continued increase in performance on Stanford Reading and Mathematics from the 8th to the 10th grades." No other group of African American students in the study—those attending magnet schools or all-Black or integrated schools in the city—showed improved performance on standardized tests between the 8th and 10th grades (Lissitz, 1993, 1994).

These findings in St. Louis, Boston, and Hartford are supported by a growing body of research on the long-term effects of desegregation on African American students (for a review, see Wells & Crain, 1994).

## SUMMARY OF THE RESEARCH ON VOLUNTARY
## TRANSFER PROGRAMS

Despite these powerful findings about the institutional and social network advantages that African American students are likely to reap in predominantly White suburban schools, we do not paint these programs as ideal, since there are many trade-offs. First of all, there is a concern about the differences in the parent involvement and advocacy between the students who transfer and those who stay behind. These issues color all three of these programs, although they are much more salient in Boston, where the informed Black parents are signing their children up for the program shortly after they are born. It is also an issue in St. Louis, despite concerted efforts to keep the program fair and open and to inform all urban Black parents of their school choices. There, we found that the parents of the students who transferred to the suburbs were much more actively involved in their children's education and much more directive and efficacious in their relationships with their sons and daughters than were the parents of the students who remained behind in the urban public schools (Wells & Crain, 1997).

Related to this concern about the students left behind is the fact that most interdistrict voluntary transfer plans do little to improve the urban schools for the students who will continue to attend them. Although the St. Louis court order included "quality" education components for the city schools, including smaller class sizes and remedial programs (Wells & Crain, 1997), such extra funding or support is unusual in these types of programs. Thus, the students and educators in the urban schools are faced not only with the stigma of being the people who were left behind, but they generally receive little support in terms of resources or development that will enable them to improve these schools.

While there is little research on the impact on these urban schools that are left behind in interdistrict voluntary transfer programs, one study of public schools less chosen in the context of the Chicago intradistrict plan argues that the teachers in these schools are discouraged and demoralized when higher-achieving students leave these schools (Easton & Bennett, 1989). In fact, the authors argue that the departure of higher-achieving students also has an impact on the remaining students. While we saw some evidence of these issues in the St. Louis public schools (see Wells & Crain, 1997, chapters 3 and 4), more systematic work on the urban schools in these three cities as well as other cities with extensive school choice policies needs to be done.

Another concern regarding these programs is the "burden of busing" issue. In these voluntary transfer programs, the burden is placed only on the Black students to create desegregated suburban schools. Thus, while the St. Louis program also includes a suburban-to-city component that allows White suburban students to attend magnet schools in the city, fewer than 1,500 White students choose to participate, while about 13,000 Black students choose to commute in the other direction (see Wells & Crain, 1997). For the most part, desegregation is taking place on the White students' cultural and social "turf." In each of these three programs, the bus rides are frequently long, which can be wearing both physically and emotionally, as Black students are required to live in two different cultural and political worlds. At the same time, opportunities for Black transfer students to socialize with suburban classmates in the evenings and on the weekends is limited. We now turn our attention to controlled choice policies.

## CONTROLLING CHOICES

Another choice-oriented school desegregation policy that came of age during the 1980s and 1990s is controlled choice. Unlike the voluntary student transfer programs, controlled choice programs are, in essence, more strictly regulated. That is, these programs find a slightly different balance between the demands of individual parents and the goal of racial integration. According to the key architects of controlled choice, Charles V. Willie and Michael Alves (1996), the philosophical foundation of this program resides in the tension between choice and control.

In its purest form, controlled choice means that every school is a school of choice and no student is automatically assigned to the nearest school. The balance is accomplished through a centralized student-assignment process that juggles parents' rank-ordered preferences with the enrollments of each school. According to Willie and Alves (1996) controlled choice has a threefold goal of school desegregation, school improvement, and choice. Controlled choice spread quickly, particularly in the Northeast, during the 1980s and early 1990s. The first controlled choice plan was established in Cambridge, Massachusetts, in 1981, in part because district officials were trying to stave off a court case that would have led to a mandatory reassignment plan.

Other cities and counties either past or present controlled choice programs include Boston, Massachusetts; East Baton Rouge, Louisiana; Fall River, Massachusetts; Indianapolis, Indiana; Lowell, Massachusetts; Montclair, New Jersey; Rockford, Illinois; San Jose, California; Saint Lucie County, Florida; Seattle, Washington; Somerville, Massachusetts; and White Plains, New York. Obviously, these cities and their school districts vary a great deal in terms of their size; thus their controlled choice programs also differ in terms of scope. For instance, in larger districts such as Boston and Saint Lucie County, the districts are divided into zones that are fairly equal in terms of the racial and social class makeup of the students within them. In these districts, the controlled choice program operates within these different zones, so that the parents in one zone have the choice of other schools within that zone. According to Willie and Alves (1996), zones should be large enough to encompass heterogeneous population groups but small enough to limit students' transportation time to no more than 40 minutes to and from school each day.

Despite variations across contexts, controlled choice plans include at least five fundamental components. First, student assignments are made according to racial-fairness guidelines, usually within a 5 to 15% range for each racial/ethnic group. Willie and Alves (1996) note that such an assignment process eliminates neighborhoods as the basis for assigning students to schools. It also creates a situation in which the racial composition of the student body in a school should not be related to whether a school is least chosen or most chosen, because all schools more or less have similar student bodies.

A second component of controlled choice plans provides for parent information centers and other outreach mechanisms to provide parents with information about the choices. These centers must be easily accessible to all parents. For example, they must be open at hours other than 9–5 and provide materials available in all appropriate languages.

A viable transportation system is the third aspect of controlled choice plans. This provision enables students to travel to schools outside their neighborhoods. The fourth component provides a school-improvement program designed to enable the least-chosen schools to become more educationally sound—places where more parents will want to enroll their children (Wells, 1993). The fifth and last component ensures the duplication of popular school programs and themes so that they are available to many parents within the district or the zone and fulfill the fairness requirement in terms of student access to good programs.

## RESEARCH EVIDENCE ON CONTROLLED CHOICE PROGRAMS

Controlled choice policies usually include strict racial-fairness guidelines, which should, theoretically, result in the schools in these districts being almost perfectly racially balanced in the context of the overall district demographics. Because these guidelines generally keep the schools within 5 to 10 percentage points of the districts' overall breakdown for each racial/ethnic group, these should be some of the most desegregated school districts in country. Unfortunately, there is little systematic research on controlled choice that can tell us the extent to which individual schools within these districts are in compliance with the fairly strict guidelines.

Another issue related to the impact of this policy on racial diversity in schools is whether the districts' overall demographics are such that meaningful racial and ethnic integration can occur. In other words, because controlled choice programs are generally implemented within the confines of single school districts, the extent to which this policy can create racially and ethnically diverse schools is dependent on the makeup of the district.

Despite the fact that many of these issues are fairly easily addressed, there is very little systematic research on them. One study of controlled choice in Rockford, Illinois (Taylor & Alves, 1999), reports some findings regarding the desegregative impact of this program during its first 2 years (1994–1996), finding that the number of segregated elementary schools in the district was reduced to 4 from at least 15 prior to the implementation of the program. In addition, no secondary school in the district had become resegregated following the implementation of the program.

Willie, Alves, and Hagerty (1996) found that in Boston, the racial distribution of students in the 33 overchosen schools was more or less the same as the distribution for the citywide public school student body—18.3% White, 45.9% African American, 25.1% Hispanic, and 10.5% Asian. In fact, they found that variations from the racial guidelines by racial/ethnic groups never varied by more than 3 percentage points in the overchosen schools. They did find, however, that there were large differences between the underchosen and the overchosen schools in terms of student drop-out and suspension rates, with underchosen schools having nearly twice the drop-out and suspension rates of overchosen schools (Willie et al., 1996).

Willie and Alves (1996) write that controlled choice programs seem to retard White flight from urban school systems. They note that in Cambridge, Massachusetts, for example, since the controlled choice program was implemented in the early 1980s, there has been a significant increase in the proportion of the school-age population in the city that attend the public schools. They note a 32% increase in new White students and a 13% increase in new minority students during a 4-year period. Rossell and Glenn (1988) also note that the proportion of school-age children living in Cambridge who attend public schools increased from 75% in 1980 to 88% in January 1986.

Similarly, Rossell and Glenn (1988) credit the controlled choice program in Cambridge for slowing the rate of White flight from the city. They also report that the racial imbalance, as measured by the Index of Dissimilarity, across the Cambridge schools declined from nearly 40 in the late 1970s to 6 in 1986. A large part of this decline occurred during 1980–81, when Cambridge also had a mandatory reassignment plan in place, but the decline continued—dropping from about 16 to 6—in the years after the mandatory plan was abandoned and the controlled choice program was in place (Rossell & Glenn, 1988).

Much of the literature on controlled choice focuses almost exclusively on the choice aspects of the policy and far less on the control aspects. In other words, authors tend to examine such issues as what percentage of parents got their first or second choice of schools (see Rossel, 1995). Yet there appears to be no mention in this literature on how many schools in a given district are within the racial-fairness guidelines.

According to Willie and Alves (1996), 80 to 85% of parents usually receive a first-choice school assignment and 85 to 90% usually receive a first-choice or second-choice school assignment. They also claim that students who receive their second-choice school assignment seldom petition to change to their first-choice school after a year attending the second-choice school.

Similarly, a 1990 report published by the Manhattan Institute found that more than 90% of students in Cambridge attend their first choice of schools, and 95% attend one of their choices (Tan, 1990, p. 11).

More specifically, in the now-defunct Boston controlled choice program, Willie and Alves (1996) report that for the 1994–95 school year, 81% of all entry-level-grade students—or those who are entering a grade such as kindergarten, sixth grade, or ninth grade in which they need to make a choice of schools—were assigned to their first choice schools. Meanwhile, they note, 90% were assigned to their either first- or second-choice schools, and 92% were assigned to one of their three top-choice schools. In a survey of parents in the Boston public schools, Willie and Alves (1996) found that 80% were either "highly satisfied" or "somewhat satisfied" with the current assignment process.

In addition, Willie and Alves (1996) cite an independent evaluation of the Boston controlled choice program that found that more than 80% of the parents were satisfied with the student-assignment process. Furthermore, when asked about their preferences for the controlled choice method of student assignment versus automatic assignment to a neighborhood school, 72% of the parents said they preferred controlled choice and the options it provided.

In Rockford, Illinois, Taylor and Alves (1999) report that 100% of all ninth-grade students and approximately 90% of all seventh-grade students have been assigned to their first-choice schools.

Still, Rossell (1995) is critical of these reports. She argues that when the data and the processes by which they are gathered are examined more carefully, a less positive picture emerges. For instance, she criticized these reports for only counting the first assignment period, not the subsequent periods, in which parents who did not make the initial deadlines, for whatever reasons, are far less likely to get their first- or second-choice schools. She also calls for the data on the percentage of parents getting their first choices to be broken down by racial groups.

Rossell (1995) also notes that the parent counseling that takes place in the controlled choice parent information centers has the effect of dissuading parents from listing their real first-choice school, especially if that school is already oversubscribed. This process of parents being counseled into the schools that their children have a good chance of getting into should be taken into account, according to Rossell, when statistics on the number of parents who get their first-choice schools are compiled. And finally, Rossell notes that parents are considered to have got their first choice when in reality their child is enrolled in their second- or third-choice school but did not move in the middle of the year when a seat became available. All these practices may contribute to inflated first-choice statistics, although no one knows by how much. Rossell writes that proponents of controlled choice believe it is minimal, while critics believe it is significant.

In short, the limited evidence regarding the impact of controlled choice programs on racial desegregation and on the right of parents to choose schools for their children is somewhat inconclusive and controversial. Still, it seems that controlled choice policies, given their universal scope and all-inclusive design, are more likely than other policies, other than mandatory reassignments, to achieve maximum racial and ethnic diversity across schools within a single school district. What is not known is whether these policies will ever be as successful in doing that in large urban school districts as they are in smaller districts that still have sizeable White populations. The recent dismantling of controlled choice programs in Boston and Seattle suggest that the challenges of implementing these programs in large and more diverse districts are great.

## CONCLUSION—WHERE DO WE GO FROM HERE?

This chapter has focused on two types of voluntary school desegregation policies—voluntary student transfer programs and controlled choice programs—that came of age in a particular moment in the history of American public education. These policies were, at one time, seen as the answer to the White and conservative backlash to the more heavy-handed mandatory student-reassignment desegregation policies. They served an important purpose by helping to create a new balance between the demands of individual parents and broader societal needs in terms of racial inequality and segregation. Thus, at one time, particularly in the late 1970s and early 1980s, these programs were models, and conservative policymakers and reformers sung their praises.

Today, despite the many successes that we have outlined in this chapter, many policymakers no longer view these programs as striking the right balance between choice and control. In the context of rapidly expanding charter school and voucher movements, voluntary school desegregation is seen as overly regulatory. The current preference among many conservatives (and even those who claim they are not so conservative) is for more deregulated, "free market" school choice programs that emphasize individual parents' "freedom of choice" over all else, with hardly a pretense of addressing broader societal issues such as racial segregation and inequality.

Meanwhile, federal courts are making it increasingly difficult for school choice policies to include any racial balance guidelines at all, placing in jeopardy all the programs we have discussed in this chapter. In 2000, the Boston public schools, for the first time in 25 years, no longer used race as a consideration in assigning students to schools. The controlled choice program implemented in Boston in the late 1980s as an alternative to the prior mandatory plan will be dismantled. According to one advocate who sued the district in an effort to end any desegregation efforts, "The race-based student-assignment policy stands in the way in reform . . . It's also illegal" (quoted in Hendrie, 1999b). Indeed, the Boston superintendent and school board opted not to defend the controlled choice program in light of recent court rulings, including one in Boston regarding the role of race in admissions to the elite exam school there.

This current policy context is particularly disconcerting in light of some of the findings suggested by the literature reviewed in this chapter—namely, that under the right conditions, school choice policies can provide students with meaningful racially desegregated school experiences that can help to create new opportunities for those students who have traditionally been most disadvantaged in the public educational system. And in the instance of controlled choice, such school choice programs can even lead to broader, systemic reform of an entire school district.

In fact, some of the most troubling findings described here are related to the more deregulatory aspects of voluntary school desegregation programs—notably that the voluntary transfer programs leave large numbers of students and educators behind in segregated urban schools that may be worse off as a result. Ironically, these are the issues and concerns that will only be exacerbated in new school choice policies that are more deregulated and are designed to address racial segregation and inequality only as an unintended consequence of "good" market-based educational reform.

# Chapter 5

# An Examination of Charter School Equity

## CAROL ASCHER and NATHALIS WAMBA

After several decades of contentious government interventions aimed at desegregating public schools and equalizing funding between urban and suburban school systems, support for government intervention on behalf of educational equality has waned in the education community—if not in our wider society. In an increasingly diverse and divided country, charter schools have entered the national policy arena, promising deregulation as a way to increase educational achievement for those students most poorly served by traditional public schools, that is, urban students of color. Indeed, many charter advocates have relocated equity in choice, and school choice for communities of color is being called an essential but "unfinished task of the civil rights movement" (Holt, 2000).

But what are the implications of charter school choice for equity? To answer this question, we begin by offering three standards of equity. Following this, we summarize equity provisions in state charter legislation. We then review research suggesting who may be choosing to send their children to charter schools and why, as well as data, including our own, on the demographic characteristics of charter school students. Finally, we discuss the challenges that charter schools pose to our traditional standards of equity.

## THREE STANDARDS OF EQUITY

In the years since *Brown*, our country has developed three standards for equity. The first, which arose as a direct consequence of the 1954 desegregation case, judges educational equity by whether there is a balanced distribution of students by race and socioeconomic status within and across schools. Since choice has represented an important departure from assigned schools, the first generation of research on charter schools has focused on whether the demographic characteristics of charter school students differ from those of students in traditional public schools in the same states and districts.

The second equity standard emerged from an understanding that, as the *Brown* court found, separate was not equal, because schools serving White students tended to be better funded and resourced than schools serving students of color. This standard judges educational equity by whether there is an equal access to high-quality learning within and across schools. In the past decades, as schools have become resegregated, this standard has been important to fiscal equity suits and other challenges to inequities across schools and districts in educational provisions that influence student achievement. While charter legislation deregulates educational processes and resources, it is important to ask whether and how this second standard is being met in charter schools.

Finally, a third equity standard asks that the distribution of student outcomes be unrelated to race/ethnicity or social-class background. This standard assumes that not all students want the same educational paths or can reach the same academic goals, but it also makes schools responsible for breaking the traditional relationship between both race/ethnicity and socioeconomic status and educational achievement. Although this may be the most difficult standard to reach, it is particularly fitting to the charter movement, which seeks autonomy over school processes in exchange for performance-based accountability.

## PROVISIONS IN CHARTER LEGISLATION
## RELATED TO EQUITY

As of 2003–2004, 41 states, the District of Columbia, and Puerto Rico have passed charter legislation enabling charter school reform. Although the charter movement has been strongly influenced by the free-market ideology of the wider choice movement, charter school legislation across the nation has also reflected regulative compromises with those concerned that the market alone may not provide equal protection for all students. Beyond the ubiquitous prohibition against discrimination in the selection of students, charter legislation in over half the states specifies that charter school students with disabilities are subject to existing state and federal laws. Seven states require charter schools to admit all eligible students and use an "equitable selection process such as lottery" in case of excess demand. About a third of the states require charter schools to reflect the racial balance of the district in which the charter school is located (RPP International, 1998). However, in no state does charter law provide an incentive for creating racially diverse schools (Wells et al., 2000). Moreover, charter law in several states gives preference to at-risk students, which affects the demography of charter schools (Jennings, Premack, Adelman, & Solomon, 1998).

On the other side, three legislative provisions indirectly influence the student populations served by charter schools and, in turn, the educational resources available to these students. First, 13 states currently allow private nonsectarian schools to convert to charter status under certain conditions. In areas where private schools serve different students from those in public schools, allowing private school conversions can affect the student populations served by charter schools.

Second, 18 states allow for-profits to sponsor charter schools, and virtually all states allow charter recipients to subcontract for-profit management companies for school facilities, curriculum, and instructional staff (RPP International, 2000). In Michigan, where management companies run 70% of all charter schools, as these companies have tried to steer clear of high-cost students, they have homogenized student enrollment and shifted their charter schools from urban to suburban areas (Miron, 2000).

Third, in only six states does charter legislation guarantee all students transportation to their charter schools (Wells et al., 2000). In some cases transportation is offered by the district; in others it is provided by the school, with the cost taken out of the school's own per-pupil revenue, constraining spending on instruction and other resources. Most often, however, it is made a parental responsibility, which means excluding from charter those students without family support.

## THE MECHANISM OF CHOICE

Influenced by market theory, choice advocates argue that parents make rational choices about where to send their children based on the quality of a school's instruction and its programmatic focus. From this perspective, parental decisions ensure that charter schools with interesting programs and high student performance survive, while those with uninteresting programs and low performance are forced to close. Market theory also assumes that information on schools can be made widely available so that *all* parents can make informed choices about both where to enroll their children and when, if necessary, to take their children out of a school. Both these assumptions have equity implications.

**Parents as Choosers**

Research on who participates in choice programs and how they select a school has been conducted in a range of contexts, including charter schools, magnet schools, interdistrict choice plans, voucher programs, and private schools. In addition there are surveys about hypothetical educational choices parents might make if they were given a choice system. Most studies focus on parents (rather than students) as decision makers; they analyze the reasons parents give for choosing—or not choosing—to send their child to a nonassigned school, where parents receive information on schools, and whether all parents have the same access to information. Since this literature has been reviewed elsewhere (see Clotfelter, 1976; Lankford & Wykoff, 2000; Lee, Croninger, & Smith, 1996; Schneider, Teske, Marschall, & Roch, 1997), we limit our analysis to choice in charter schools.

Several studies of how urban parents choose charter schools suggest that educational quality is key to parents, with the school's philosophy, size, and safety following closely in importance. Horn and Miron (1999) surveyed 981 parents in urban settings in Michigan to find out why they enrolled their child in a charter school. Parents gave the following six factors their top rating, with a score of 5 representing most important: "good teachers and high-quality instruction" (4.32), "emphasis and philosophy of this school" (4.27), "safety for my child" (4.15), "academic reputation of school" (4.02), "more emphasis on academic than extracurricular activities" (3.79), and "promises made by charter school's spokespersons" (3.59).

For parents in Washington, DC, the most frequently mentioned reason (68%) for parents' choosing a charter school was the school's academic quality. More than a third of the parents also cited religious instruction and school discipline. More than a quarter of parents reported class size, teacher quality, and school safety as critical to their choice of a school.

In answer to a questionnaire offering charter school parents possible reasons for having chosen a charter school, more than half of all parents checked "small size" (53%); this was followed by "higher standards"

(45.9%), "educational philosophy" (44.0%), "greater opportunity for parent involvement" (43.0%), and "better teachers" (41.9%). However, there were interesting variations by social class. While nearly 50% of the upper-income respondents agreed that they had chosen the charter school because its program was "closer to my philosophy," only 37.2% of all low-income parents gave this reason. Conversely, while 42% of all low-income parents rated the convenience of the charter school's location as important, only 13.4% of all upper-income respondents rated this reason as important (Finn, Manno, & Vanourek, 2000).

Even when low-income families desire school choice, and value a strong academic curriculum, they may not make their decisions based on the same amount or kind of information as do families with greater economic resources. Smrekar and Goldring (1999) found that high-income families tended to have access to, and to utilize, a wider array of resources than low-income parents when choosing a school. Those parents with the least access to resources were those who were out of work and had never graduated from high school or attended college.

*Texas Open-Enrollment Charter Schools: Third Year Evaluation* (2000) of Texas charter schools, which included at-risk charter schools serving predominantly students of color and academic charter schools serving predominantly White students, reports interesting differences by race/class in whether parents are involved in choosing their children schools. While nearly half (45.6%) of the students of color attending charter schools serving at-risk students made the choice on their own; just a fifth (21.5%) of the Anglo students attending the academic charter schools had decided on their own. Yet only 9% of the students attending at-risk schools said the family made the decision without their input, while 29.9% of the students in the academic charter schools were there solely because of their family's decision. More than three quarters of both groups indicated that the most important reason for choosing a charter school was their belief that the school offered "classes that best fit the students' needs" (Barrett et al., 1997). However, the fact that Anglo students were in academically oriented charter schools and minority students in vocational programs would justify inquiring about the meaning of "classes that best fit the students' needs," as well as how well informed students and their parents are about the quality of school programs when making a school choice.

## Schools as Choosers

Within the context of state legislation, charter schools have a developed variety of recruitment and admission policies that influence who learns about the school, who applies, and who is accepted or rejected. Thus, schools are also involved in choice.

The first national study of charter schools used a telephone survey to ask charter school staff about their admissions processes. Nearly three quarters of all respondents reported that applications had exceeded admissions, and so necessitated some selection policy on their part. Of the schools with excess demand, 39% reported using a lottery or other random process to allocate admissions; 41% used a "first come, first served" policy; and 10% used a combination. Just fewer than 10% used other processes, including referral from the courts or social services (RPP International & the University of Minnesota, 1997). As others have noted, a first come, first served policy easily disadvantages those with less or later information (Levin, 2000; Wells et al., 2000). Moreover, since admissions are still dependent on who applies, random processes alone may not ensure racial balance in charter schools.

To recruit students, charter schools use recommending by word of mouth, advertising to targeted groups, mailing to selected constituents, posting flyers in local communities, and advertising in local newspapers. Some charter schools send their representatives to attend meetings of potential parents or to make presentations about their schools (Wells, 2000). All these methods target particular students and their families at the expense of others. For example, in Michigan some charter schools have used marketing strategies to make themselves especially available and attractive to members of particular ethnic or racial groups. In districts where most of the students are minorities, the target market has often been White students (Arsen, Plank, & Sykes, 1999).

Beyond these factors influencing recruitment and selection, a curricular focus can act as an informal but strong selection devise. For example, a school with an Afrocentric, Hispanic, or Islamic cultural focus will attract African Americans or Latinos, or immigrants from the Middle East, respectively. By contrast, a number of charter schools have discovered that their small size and student-centered instruction draw more troubled students then they had anticipated (Ascher et al., 2000; Horn & Miron, 1999).

## CHARTER SCHOOL DEMOGRAPHY

The U.S. Department of Education's Office of Educational Research and Improvement has sponsored four national studies of charter schools. The two most recent national studies, the third- and fourth-year reports (RPP International, 1999, 2000), cover 678 charter schools in 24 states, or 94%

of the charter schools in 27 states operating in 1997–98, and 1,011 charter schools, or 94% of those operating in 27 states in 1998–99. Comparing the two most recent reports, we can surmise several interesting changes in charter school demography. First, the percentage of White students in charter schools had declined from 55% in 1997–98 to about 48 percent in 1998–99. While in the earlier report, six states (Connecticut, Massachusetts, Michigan, Minnesota, North Carolina, and Texas) enrolled a much higher percentage of students of color than did all public schools, a year later, three additional states (Louisiana, Illinois, and New Jersey) were enrolling a much higher percentage of students of color in charter schools than in all public schools. However, in both years charter schools in Alaska, California, and Georgia enrolled a higher percentage of White students than did the public schools.

Second, the percentage of low-income charter students had remained at 37%, slightly under the average for all public schools (39%). Third, the percentage of English-language learners (LEPs) students enrolled in charter schools had remained at 10%, about the same as in all public schools, and the percentage of students with disabilities stayed at 8%, several percentage points lower than in all public schools (RPP International, 1999, 2000).

## THE IESP ANALYSIS OF CHARTER SCHOOLS AND THEIR DISTRICTS

Our charter school research team at New York University's Institute for Education and Social Policy (IESP) was concerned that early national analyses of charter school demography made equity statements based on comparisons of charter schools with state and even national public school populations. Thus, in 1998, we began to collect our own demographic data. Our IESP database includes 801 charter schools operating in 1997–98. Data on these schools contain information on student ethnicity, as well as percentage of students eligible for free or reduced lunch programs, percentage of LEPs, and percentage receiving special education services. In addition, a linked IESP database includes comparative demographic data (student ethnicity, free or reduced-price lunch, and so on) for the 33 public school districts and the 26 states in which our 801 charter schools are located.

While we were beginning our own analysis, using 1997–98 data, the RPP released its second-year report, which also compared charter schools and the geographic districts in which they were located used 1996–97. This report is the only one to have presented such a detailed analysis of the students served by charter schools. Unfortunately, districts themselves may represent averages of a number of schools that vary widely in their demography. Thus, the charter-school-versus-district comparisons conducted by the RPP, as well as the analysis that follows, do not tell us where the charter schools stand within their districts' demographic range.

Following RPP, we determined whether charter schools are distinct from their districts by measuring whether the population of White students is within 20% (greater or less than) of the average percentage of White students in the district. While the RPP found 60% of all charter schools to be indistinct from their districts in the percentage of White students served in 1996–97, our data from a year later (1997–98) suggests that 70% of all charter schools are not distinct from their surrounding districts in the percentage of White students. (RPP International's third-year report also found 70% to be indistinct from their districts.)

However, we also sought to understand under what demographic conditions charter schools were most likely to look like their districts. We found that in about half the charter schools in our sample (52%), more than two thirds of the students are White; 83% of these predominantly White charters are indistinct from their district averages. However, in 31% of all charter schools, more than two thirds of the students are of color; more than half (53%) of these schools serving predominantly students of color are indistinct from their district averages.

Thus, although most charter schools look like their districts, it is also clear that the higher the percentage of White students in the charter schools, the more likely charter schools are to be indistinct from their districts (within 20% of the district average of White students). However, nearly half of all charter schools with more than two thirds students of color are distinct from their districts. That is, charter schools may be offering students of color a more segregated environment than their districts as a whole.

In Table 5.1, we present IESP data to show some of this variation in charter schools and their surrounding districts.

As the charter school bar graph shows, the largest numbers of charter schools lie at the far ends of the spectrum, where White students constitute either 0–20% or 81–100% of the student population. By contrast, the district bar graph shows that there are more districts with higher percentages of White students. That is, although charter schools are more likely to be situated in predominantly White districts, nearly a quarter of the charter schools for which we have data serve 80% or more students of color.

Because ethnicity does not necessarily overlap with social class, we

**Table 5.1.** Concentration of White Students in Charter Schools and Related Public School Districts, 1997–98 IESP Data

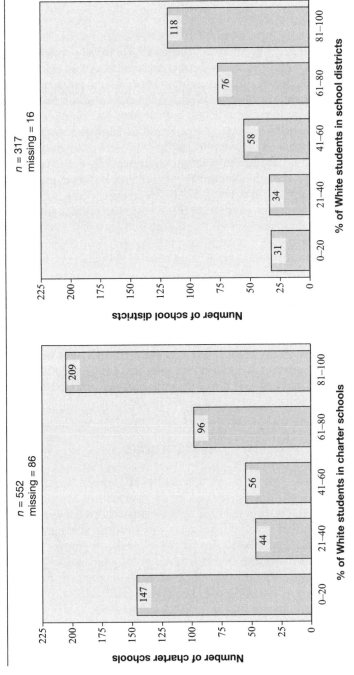

also sought to determine to what extent charter schools are serving low-income students. The two bar graphs in Table 5.2, both based on IESP data, explain the differences between charter schools and their districts in the percentage of students eligible for free and reduced-price lunch.

In this case, we have subdivided the first quintile to show that 163, or a third of all charter schools, had *no* students eligible for free or reduced-price lunches. (We believe that this high percentage may result from the schools' reluctance to participate in the program, and so their disinterest in accurately calculating eligibility.) By comparison, only two districts had no students eligible for free and reduced-price lunches. At the other end of the spectrum, 52 (10.7%) charter schools have more than 80% of their students eligible for free and reduced-price lunch, compared with 14 districts (4.5%) with more than 80% of their student population eligible for free and reduced-price lunch.

In short, our data suggest that charter schools may be proliferating at both the low and the high end of the race/ethnicity and affluence/poverty continuums. It is likely that some schools serving high percentages of students of color are responding to legislation that asks charter schools to serve at-risk students. We believe that it is also likely that charter schools are serving more low-income students than the free- and reduced-price lunch eligibility data suggest. Although our data cannot show that charter schools are exacerbating racial isolation, or creating more isolation by social class among students, the state-level research described below suggests this to be the case.

## STATE STUDIES

Over the past several years, a number of states have conducted their own analyses of the students served by charter schools. Several make for particularly interesting studies, both because charter school laws in these states grant high levels of autonomy (including the absence of equity provisions and the possibility of private schools converting to charter status) and because the investigations go beyond mere demography to look at the relationship between the students served and the instructional resources offered in the charter schools.

Arizona's charter legislation, passed in 1994, is still considered the most deregulated in the United States and is said to have created a "virtual voucher system." Arizona also has more charter schools than any other state—in 1999, 222 charter schools enrolled 815,388 students, or 4% of the total public school population in the state (RPP International,

**Table 5.2.** Charter Schools and Their Districts Free and Reduced-Price Lunch

2000). The law allows private schools to convert to charter status; 29 charter schools in Arizona were formerly private schools.

An analysis of charter schools in Arizona (Cobb & Glass, 1999) compared the ethnic compositions of 55 urban and 57 rural charter schools to their public school neighbors. Nearly half the charter schools exhibited evidence of "substantial ethnic separation"—that is, segregation by race/ethnicity. Moreover, Arizona's charter schools were 20% higher in White enrollment than other public schools. Cobb and Glass conclude, "The degree of ethnic separation in Arizona schools is large enough and consistent enough to warrant concern among education policymakers" (1999, p. 2).

As important, charter schools serving a majority of ethnic minority students tended to be either vocational secondary schools that do not lead to college or "schools of last resort" for students expelled from traditional public schools. Charter schools with college-bound curricula catered primarily to White students (Cobb & Glass, 1999).

In California, charter school legislation, which was passed in 1992, has made local school districts the major grantors of charters. Although some charter advocates have feared that districts would be reluctant to grant charters, the state now hosts 149 charter schools, or nearly 10% of all charters in the United States. The law states that the reform is to increase learning opportunities for all students, with a special emphasis on those identified as low achievers, and every school's chartering document must describe the means by which the school will achieve racial/ethnic balance reflective of the sponsor district. However, research on California charter schools suggests that neither the state nor the districts are monitoring charter school for equity compliance (Wells, 2000; RPP International, 1998).

In 1997, just less than half of all charter school students were White, compared with 40% of all public school students. Latinos constituted 34% of all charter school students, compared to 40% in the public school system, and African American students constituted 9% in both types of schools. The authors believe that "at least part of this discrepancy reflects patterns of residential segregation, as opposed to any efforts on the part of charter schools to be exclusionary" (SRI International, 1997, pp. 11–13).

The UCLA Charter School Study (1998), which focused on 17 charter schools in 10 California districts, found that in many conversion charter schools the student populations remained the same as they had been when the schools were traditional public schools. However, in 10 of the 17 schools under study, at least one racial or ethnic group was over- or underrepresented by 15% or more in comparison with their district racial makeup. As in the SRI study, White students were overrepresented in charter schools (by 8% statewide), while Latino students were underrepresented (by 6% statewide). Wells also found the same percentage of African American students in the public schools and charter schools.

Charter school legislation in Michigan, which was passed in 1993, has enabled the creation of 124 "public school academies" in the state. The state law is among the most permissive with regard to a diversity among organizers and sponsors (authorizers) of charter schools, the legal independence of charter schools, and the deregulation of collective bargaining requirements. Twenty-six of Michigan's charter schools were formerly nonsectarian private schools, and for-profit educational management companies currently run 63 schools. Although charter school legislation prohibits discrimination in admissions, it does not include any provision for racial or ethnic balance (Mintrom & Plank, 2000; Public Sector Consultants & MAXIMUS, 1999).

Michigan has also adopted an open-enrollment policy that allows students to transfer to charter schools and other public schools in neighboring school districts, as long as there is space (Mintrom & Plank, 2000; RPP International, 1998). A recent Michigan State University study focused on the impact of charter schools and open-enrollment plans on schools and school districts (Arsen, Plank, & Sykes, 1999). The authors noted that while a trend toward social separation in the public school systems in Michigan did not originate with school choice policies, the introduction of such policies may well accelerate this trend toward separation.

An evaluation of 55 Michigan charter schools—more than half what the sample was in Detroit—categorized them in three groups. General schools, constituting 51% of the sample, offer a curriculum targeted to the general population of students. Ethnocentric schools, offering an ethnic-based curriculum, such as Armenian, African American, or Latino, constitute 13% of all charter schools. Specialty schools, serving specific populations of students such as youth returning from incarceration, students who have dropped out, and youth with mental impairment, constitute 36% of all charter schools. Because of the preponderance of Detroit schools in the study, the racial composition of the 55 charter schools was 69.3% African American, compared with only 14% African American in the general Michigan population (Public Sector Consultants & MAXIMUS, 1999).

Public Sector Consultants and MAXIMUS report that teachers in the charter schools investigated were younger and had less teaching experience than teachers in traditional public schools. The average salary for charter school teachers was lower ($29,178) than that of teachers in traditional public schools (the statewide figure is $47,181). However, the average pupil-teacher ratio was slightly lower than the statewide average: 19.2:1 versus 21.8:1 in school year 1997–98. Finally, charter schools experienced serious disadvantages in revenue. In 1997–98, the per pupil grant for the Dearborn School District, for example, was $7,556, but charter schools in the same district received $5,962 per pupil—about 21% less. The state average was $6,061 (Horn & Miron, 1999).

Given the divergence between the charter school enrollment and the demography of the entire state, differences between resources in charter schools and other public schools may also have a racial effect, with African American students being served by less resourced charter schools than White students in public schools.

In Texas, charter school legislation provides for the creation of a limited number of open-enrollment charter schools serving traditional students, and an unlimited number of charter schools serving 75% or more students classified as at risk. In the 1998–99 academic year, 89 charter schools served a population of 17,616 students. Forty-three schools were classified as at-risk schools and 40 as non-at-risk schools. Six schools did not provide the percentage of at-risk students served (Weiher, 1999). Because of the large number of charter schools serving at-risk students, Texas charter schools have higher percentages of students of color and lower percentages of Anglo students than the state's public school system. However, non-at-risk charter schools also have much lower concentrations of students of color and slightly higher concentrations of Anglo students than both non-at-risk charter schools and other Texas public schools.

At-risk charter schools also have a much higher proportion of noncertified teachers (62.3% versus 47.5%) and a slightly higher proportion of nondegree teachers (11.7% versus 10.5%) than do non-at-risk schools. The teacher-student ratio is also much higher in at-risk charter schools than in non-at-risk charter schools—1:24.9 versus 1:17.8 (Weiher, 1999).

Since choice has represented an important departure from assigned schools, the initial generation of research on charter schools has focused on racial balance, the first standard of equity. As our chapter shows, there is some evidence nationally that charter schools may further racial and economic isolation. Although charter schools are so diverse that broad conclusions may obscure both good and bad news about their effects on equity, there is also state evidence relating to the second equity standard: It suggests that, at a minimum, charter schools are not decreasing the resource inequities that have plagued traditional public schools.

Instead, existing evidence points to inequities in resources between charter schools serving low-income students of color and those serving White middle-class students.

## CHARTER SCHOOL EQUITY

Charter reform has shifted the notion of equality to a market vision of equality. Rather than similar schools being delivered to heterogeneous populations of students, schools are now to be directed at particular clienteles, and equity is to be found in the match between students' needs and the specific educational program provided (Finn et al., 2000).

Several serious questions arise from what might be considered a newly developing vision of equity as differentiation. First, is instruction in charter schools really being differentiated to suit the specific learning needs of individual students? Or are programs being developed to appeal to different clientele—Afrocentric or Native American curriculum—en masse? (A classroom of African American or Native American students will include students who learn quite differently.) More problematic are educators and private management companies making pedagogical decisions that disadvantage at-risk and other low-income and low-performing students. Studies of charter schools in several states suggest a crude programmatic and curricula differentiation between schools serving White middle-class students and low-income students of color. If this is not the "one best system," it is also not an education directed to helping each individual child "thrive" and "blossom."

Our own fieldwork in urban charter schools suggests that some charter schools may well have developed educational programs that draw a range of students, and so have managed to desegregate without regulations and mandates. (These may be both educationally sound and low-quality schools.) Although we have more than two decades of experience with magnet schools, we still know relatively little about what types of curricula and instructional programs are most likely to generate desegregation. This would be very relevant information to the charter movement, which promises both differentiation and desegregation without the regulation for racial balance under which magnets operate.

Some urban charter schools are also providing high-quality educational opportunities to low-income children of color in segregated environments. In these cases, the charter schools meet our second standard of equity. Unfortunately, the state studies we review suggest that more often charter schools serving low-income children of color are less likely to provide an academic curriculum than are charter schools serving White middle-class students and are generally not as rich in educational resources.

The third equity standard, focused on outcomes, is particularly fitting to the charter movement, which seeks freedom from the regulation of inputs and processes in exchange for performance-based accountability. This standard assumes that not all students want the same educational paths or can reach the same academic goals, but it also assumes that schools are responsible for breaking the traditional relationship between both race/ethnicity and socioeconomic status and educational achievement. Until now, it has been difficult to obtain any cross-school analysis of charter school achievement. Nevertheless, we can posit that by this third equity standard, the charter movement will have achieved educational equity when there are no differences in achievement between urban and nonurban charter schools and when the race/ethnicity and the social class of the students served show no ability to predict achievement outcomes.

# Chapter 6

# Steering Toward Separation

## The Policy and Legal Implications of "Counseling" Special Education Students Away from Charter Schools

KEVIN G. WELNER and KENNETH R. HOWE

Inclusion is a guiding principle of special education in the United States. As codified in the Individuals with Disabilities Education Act (IDEA), students with disabilities are entitled to a free, appropriate public education in the least restrictive environment (LRE) (20 U.S.C. §§ 1400, *et seq.*). The meaning of this LRE mandate is clear as applied to heterogeneous schools: Students with disabilities shall be placed in mainstream classes whenever educationally appropriate. In a multifaceted choice system, however, this placement step occurs subsequent to a school selection process—a process that holds the potential to greatly undermine inclusion—especially considering the multiple state legislative contexts. In particular, admissions processes can effectively filter out students with disabilities.

In this chapter we examine the mounting evidence that choice schools, particularly charter schools, are steering away students with disabilities. *Steering away* generally refers to the discouragement of students with disabilities at the preenrollment or enrollment phase, while *counseling out* refers to attempts to convince already enrolled students with disabilities to leave the school. In this chapter, we use *steering away*, or simply *steering*, broadly, encompassing both phenomena. We investigate how choice schools have responded to market forces by favoring traditionally abled students over special needs students, the most severe of whom are often students of color. In light of this past response, we consider the tension between various goals underlying the movement toward choice schools, and we conclude with a brief discussion of possible modifications of the legal and policy framework that could result in more equitable options for special needs students.

## THE LEGAL FRAMEWORK FOR SPECIAL EDUCATION AND CHOICE SCHOOLS

Special education is a statutory creation, as are choice schools. The federal IDEA, along with state statutes, frame special education. The legal creation of choice schools is less uniform. Charter schools, for instance, are framed primarily by each state's enabling legislation, although recent federal legislation also includes several mandates (such as an admissions lottery) attached to charter school funding. The legal relationship between choice schools and students with disabilities involves federal disability laws, state special education statutes, state legislation creating and governing choice schools, and policies and rules from state education agencies (SEAs) and local education agencies (LEAs). All these authorities, as interpreted by courts and regulatory authorities, interact to create the legal environment for special education and school choice.

While IDEA provides the most comprehensive legal structure to protect the educational rights of students with disabilities, two antidiscrimination laws also provide important protection. Section 504 of the Rehabilitation Act of 1973 (29 U.S.C. § 794) and Title II of the Americans with Disabilities Act (42 U.S.C. §§ 12101, *et seq.*) prohibit discrimination based on disability in the administration of public services, including education. Section 504 and Title II contain similar language, offer similar protections, and have similar court interpretations (Losen & Welner, 2001).

In a nutshell, the nondiscrimination provisions in Section 504 and Title II require that choice schools must make reasonable accommodations as necessary to serve students with disabilities. Accommodations are considered reasonable unless they would create "undue hardship" to the LEA or would "fundamentally alter the nature" of the school's services or program. This provision means that a school with an accepted test-score admission process could exclude students who score low on the test, even if this disproportionately burdens students with disabilities, while a back-to-basics school could not set academic criteria, such as reading at grade level, because it is not necessary to fulfill the school's mission (Heubert, 1997). As we shall see, enforcement of these provisions must strike a balance between protecting legitimate interests and creating a loophole that operators of choice schools can either intentionally or unwittingly abuse.

Heubert (1997) warns that a charter school must admit a special education student as long as it is capable of providing appropriate services. The *school* must adapt; it cannot demand that the *student* adapt. The school is obliged to provide all services in the existing individualized education program (IEP) and to inform the parent of the right to continue receiving all those services.

As a general rule, LEAs are free to create cost-saving mechanisms that concentrate special education resources at particular sites. However, this is allowed only when the mechanisms do not deny unique educational opportunities to the special education child and that such concentration does not violate a student's IEP or IDEA inclusion mandates. Choice schools that would like to avoid special education students are therefore faced with a dilemma. Their claimed *raison d'être* is their uniqueness, and it ill behooves them to argue that another public school could provide the same educational experience. So their uniqueness obligates them to admit students whom they would otherwise discourage.

Accordingly, Heubert (1997) argues that the range of choice available to students with disabilities in such schools must be comparable with that offered to other students. Choice schools, to the extent that they fulfill their promise of being unique and innovative, "have less leeway to deny admission to students with disabilities or to achieve economies of scale through clustering or cooperative arrangements with other schools" (p. 346). Disabled students must be provided with equal access and opportunities; a unique choice school would appear to represent such an opportunity.

Some charter school advocates contend that parents sometimes seek out charter schools precisely because they do not want the special labeling and treatment of normal public schools (Vanourek, Manno, Finn, & Bierlein, 1997). However, such discussions between parents and charter schools must be premised on a clear understanding of these rights. The parent, Heubert (1997) explains, must be "fully aware of the child's rights" and must freely choose, "without any coercion, however subtle" to forgo the evaluation or services (p. 326). Thus, choice schools providing educational services to "handicapped" children who are not receiving services under IDEA are nonetheless entitled to protection under the Section 504 regulations (Ahearn, 1999).

### IDEA and Charter Schools Legislation

Until 1997, federal legislation did not address the relationship between charter schools and students with disabilities. The IDEA regulations did, however, broadly mandate state responsibility for guaranteeing nondiscriminatory and complete schooling of children with disabilities.

The 1997 reauthorization of IDEA adds the requirement that SEAs and LEAs ensure that students with disabilities attending charter schools will be served in the same manner as that of any other child with a disability in any other type of public school. The regulations mandate that IDEA applies to all public agencies, including public charter schools, no matter whether they are (a) established as an free-standing LEA under state laws, (b) not included as LEAs or educational service agencies (ESAs), or (c) not a school of an LEA or ESA (34 C.F.R. §§300.18, 300.22). Moreover, charter students and their parents retain the same rights under IDEA that they would have in a noncharter public school, regardless of whether the charter school receives funding through IDEA (34 C.F.R. §300.312(a)).

These regulations provide that a charter school that is an LEA and receives IDEA funding must maintain responsibility for ensuring that the law's requirements are met. These duties include the receipt of services in accordance with a properly developed IEP, plus the meeting of all procedural safeguards such as parental consent and prior written notice. If a charter is not an LEA but is a school of an LEA that receives IDEA funds, then the LEA must ensure that these statutory requirements are met and must serve the children with disabilities attending the charter school, passing along IDEA funding to the charter school in the same manner that it does for other schools. If a charter is neither an LEA nor a school of an LEA that receives IDEA funds, then the SEA is responsible for ensuring that the requirements are met by that school.

Each SEA remains ultimately responsible for complying with IDEA's substantive and procedural requirements. The SEA must ensure that a free, appropriate public education (FAPE) is available to all children with disabilities and that these students are educated, to the maximum extent appropriate, with nondisabled children. The SEA must further ensure that children with disabilities and their parents are afforded the procedural protections set forth in IDEA. This is true of children in charter schools as well as those attending traditional public schools, and no state school-choice legislation has the legal authority to exempt schools or SEAs from these federal obligations.

The two IDEA provisions that choice schools find most nettlesome require that disabled students must be (a) placed in the LRE, meaning that they must be included in regular classrooms and other settings with nondisabled students to the maximum extent appropriate (20 U.S.C. §1412[a][5] and 34 C.F.R. §300.550[b][1]); and (b) taught by personnel who are "appropriately and adequately prepared and trained" and who meet the "highest standard in the state" for the provisions of special education (34 C.F.R. §300.136). The federal mandate, therefore, is only that special education students in charter schools have teachers who meet the same minimum standards that a state sets for other public school special education teachers.

Because most charter school founders, teachers, and parents relish their independence and freedom, these rules are a particularly bitter pill for them to swallow (Coeyman, 2001; Lange & Lehr, 2000). Vanourek and colleagues (1997) write of a "vexing dilemma" whereby charter schools "are required by law to follow special-ed laws as regular schools do, but what often makes them appealing is that they approach these matters differently."

This different "approach" for some charter schools has included un-derserving special education students or steering them away. Moreover, IDEA's rules simply represent a vision of meaningful education for students with disabilities, and most expenses and other burdens associated with providing such an education would exist even without IDEA. That is, IDEA's educational rationale, not its corresponding regulatory framework, accounts for many of its burdens and for the underlying motivation of steering. Students with disabilities will, as a group, be more expensive and present more "challenging behaviors" and "significant learning problems" (McLaughlin, Henderson, & Ullah, 1996, p. 9).

## Charter School Legislation

Although the legislation allowing for charter schools (the so-called enabling legislation) differs from state to state, the general framework is consistent. Charter schools are exempt from many restrictions and bureaucratic rules that govern traditional schools. They must nonetheless abide by all federal (and most state) laws addressing safety, health, and civil rights, including federal disability laws. Thus, the bulk of their increased autonomy concerns relief from state statutes and regulations governing the areas of budgeting, curriculum and instruction, materials, schedules, facilities, and personnel. Regarding personnel, fewer teachers in charter schools may need to be certified (depending on the state), although certification of special education teachers may be required (depending on the state and on the interpretation of federal disability law).

Generally speaking, state special education laws ignore charter schools, and state charter school laws ignore special education (Ahearn, 1999). The following legislative overview focuses on the few provisions that do offer assistance, relying heavily on Fiore and Cashman (1998), and demonstrates that the state legislative context as it relates to special education can have direct influence on the steering away of those students from charter schools in a given state.

Legislative provisions that most directly concern the issue of steering expressly prohibit discrimination in admissions based on disability. Eighteen states include such a provision. Four additional states have a provision that prohibits discrimination against protected individuals in any context, presumably including admissions. Eight states that have an admissions nondiscrimination clause also have a general nondiscrimination clause.

Notwithstanding these nondiscrimination provisions, several states allow charter schools to establish enrollment criteria consistent with the school's mission or scope, or to limit enrollment to a specialized area or focus (Ahearn, 1999). Some of these states—such as New Hampshire and Texas—specifically permit admissions based on academic-achievement criteria. Nine states forbid the use of such criteria, while two others warn against unreasonable or sole reliance on such criteria. More proactively (but less enforceably), the laws in eight states expressly provide that a primary purpose of the charter school legislation is to offer increased learning opportunities for special populations. The legislation in some of these states uses general terms, while two states specifically name students with disabilities as a target population.

Finally, four states' charter school statutes include provisions designed to ensure that the schools enroll a cross-section of the community's students; however, only two of these states specifically include special education students in their provision. Louisiana and Rhode Island have provisions that include special education students. The laws in New Jersey and North Carolina focus instead on racial or academic factors. Other provisions that demonstrate an increased focus on target populations (but not specifically special education populations) include Colorado's requirement that a certain number of charter schools focus on target populations and Texas's relaxation of restrictions on the total number of open-enrollment charter schools for schools focusing on target populations. In addition, three state statutes (in California, Connecticut, and Massachusetts) require reports with respect to special populations within their charter schools.

## EVIDENCE OF STEERING

To date, no published research has reported a systematic large-scale study of steering phenomena. However, over the past 6 years an increasing amount of published research has described troubling instances and practices. These anecdotal reports, grounded either on larger studies of choice schools (where steering was noted even though it was not the main focus of the study; see McLaughlin, Henderson, & Ullah, 1996; Arsen, Plank, & Sykes, 1999) or in case studies of individual schools (see Zollers & Ramathan, 1998), offer documentation to support the hypothesis that schools will react in predictable, discriminatory ways in response to competition, accountability pressures, and assertions of parental autonomy.

In the remainder of this section, we first discuss the enrollment evidence indicating that some choice schools are steering away special education students. We then discuss three incentives for choice schools to steer away special education students—finances, accountability, and homogenizaton—and the evidence that they are responding to these incentives. Finally, we describe the means of steering special education students away that have been employed by choice schools.

### Patterns of Enrollment

Ahearn, Lange, Rhim, & McLaughlin (2001) conducted two comprehensive studies on the statewide enrollment of special education students in 15 states. The Department of Education surveyed 23 states, finding in 15 states and the District of Columbia that charter schools enrolled a lower percentage of special education students than traditional public schools. In 15 states and the District of Columbia, the percentage of special education students enrolled in charter schools was lower than the percentage enrolled in the public schools. This group included all the jurisdictions with the largest charter school movements relative to the number of public education students served. Against this general trend, seven states enrolled a larger percentage of special education students in charter schools than in public schools. Each of these states has a small to mid-sized charter school movement.

Ahearn et al. (2001) conducted in-depth interviews with key informants in each of the 15 states studied, concluding that "there is some 'counseling out' of students with disabilities" (p. 27).

In addition to this large-scale survey study, more focused research of the effects of various state choice systems on special needs students is beginning to accumulate—typically from states that have significant charter school programs under way. The findings confirm the claim suggested in the Department of Education survey that school choice is resulting in the stratification and exclusion of special needs students. Interestingly, some charter schools have been found to enroll a disproportionate number of special needs students, while others have virtually none (Center for Applied Research and Educational Improvement, 1998; Lange, 1997).

For instance, in his examination of Arizona's 46 charter schools operating during the 1995–96 school year, McKinney (1996) found that only 4% of children enrolled in these schools were receiving special education services, compared with a statewide rate of 10%. In Colorado, an analysis conducted by McLaughlin and colleagues (1996) concluded that charter schools were serving a lesser proportion of students with disabilities than were schools statewide (7.31% as compared with 9.09%). A more recent study by the Colorado Department of Education (2002, p. 49) identified an even wider gap: 5.9% as compared with 9.8%.

Texas, where, like Colorado, the charter school legislation is designed to favor service of at-risk populations, shows similar disparities. As Lance Fusarelli reports on his study of Texas charter schools:

> Only 9 percent of students enrolled in charter schools are classified as Special Education compared with a state average of 12 percent; only 3 percent of students in charter schools are LEP compared to a state average of 12 percent. . . . Since at least half of charter schools in Texas are created to meet the needs of students most at-risk of dropping out (a point made by advocates of charter schools), enrollment of special education and LEP students in charter schools in Texas should be *higher* than the statewide average. (2000, p. 7; emphasis in original).

Good and Braden (2000), discussing national trends, reported, "Some charter schools exclude special education students altogether; others educate a majority of special education students, effectively segregating them from less-restrictive forms of education; and still others accept only special education students with less-severe disabilities" (p. 19). Garn (2000) reported that Arizona charter schools spent considerably less on special education than did public schools in the state, 1.4% versus 10%. Furthermore, a very few charter schools spent a considerable amount on special needs students, whereas nearly half spent nothing at all. These figures on allocations for special needs students provide strong, albeit indirect, evidence that Arizona charter schools are excluding special needs students on a massive scale. Similarly, Arsen and colleagues (1999), in their study of Michigan, concluded that the few charter schools enrolling special education students provided less costly services, and in 1997–1998, 75% of the schools provided no services at all.

In California, little difference was found in the proportion of special education students enrolled in charter schools versus ordinary public schools overall. However, when newly formed, "start-up" charter schools were distinguished from public schools that converted to charters ("conversion" charter schools), the difference was pronounced. Whereas 26% of start-up charter schools had no special education students, only 6% of conversion charters had none (SRI International, 1997, reported in the UCLA Charter School Study, 1998).

As the California study suggests, general enrollment statistics can mask what only finer distinctions can reveal. A choice school may report, for example, a 10% special education student population. However, these students may not reflect the distribution of student disabilities in that school's district. Zollers and Ramathan (1998) found this to be the case with regard to for-profit charters in Massachusetts. They found that, as compared to the respective local school districts, for-profit charter schools had a distribution of special education students that was weighted (using Massachusetts's scale from .1 to .8) toward more .1 and .2 students and fewer .3 and .4 students. Zollers and Ramathan concluded, "While they have done a decent job of including students with mild disabilities, for-profit charter schools in Massachusetts have engaged in a pattern of disregard and often blatant hostility toward students with more complicated behavioral and cognitive disabilities" (Zollers & Ramathan, 1998, p. 298; see also Rhim & McLaughlin, 2000, p. 25).

Colorado provides another example of how general enrollment statistics can mask the true picture. Charter schools enroll 5.9% special education students on average, whereas the districts in which they are located enroll 9.8% on average. But this substantial gap encompasses even larger gaps for certain types of charter schools. For instance, the most prevalent curriculum model employed by Colorado's charter schools, by far, is E. D. Hirsch's Core Knowledge curriculum. Almost all these schools enroll a smaller percentage of special education students than do the districts in which they are located. In the few cases in which they exceed the district average (2 of 21) it is by a small margin, and these districts have lower than the state average of special education students. These Core Knowledge charter schools enroll an average of 4.6% special education students; the average for the districts in which they are located is 8.9%. Thus, whereas Colorado's charter schools as a whole enroll roughly two thirds (65%) of the percentage of special education students in the districts in which they are located, its Core Knowledge charter schools enroll roughly one half (52%) (Colorado Department of Education, 2000). The pattern here is one of separation. Some charter schools, particularly those focused on serving special needs populations, enroll relatively high numbers of special education students, while others enroll very low numbers. According to the U.S. Department of Education (2000), "Across states, the percentage of students with disabilities served by charter schools continued to vary significantly, in part because a higher proportion of charter schools in some states were specifically designed to serve this population of students." While one may praise those charter schools reaching out to special education and other at-risk populations, the overall stratifying effect of specialized choice schools does nothing to further the broader goal of inclusion.

In summary, two general trends are exhibited in patterns of choice school special education enrollment: (a) special education students are enrolling in choice schools in lower percentages than in public schools overall, and (b) further layers of stratification lie beneath the surface that may be associated with approaches that certain choice schools adopt for themselves.

Public schools have, over the past quarter century, enrolled special education students based on catchment areas, resulting in a relatively even distribution of such students among schools. In contrast, choice schools appear to be distributing these students in a more uneven way, such that many of these schools serve few or no special education students. Furthermore, the growing choice movement holds the potential to drive greater racial segregation among the general student population and particularly among students with special needs. Minority students tend to be overrepresented in certain categories of disability while underrepresented in others. As a general rule, classifications that carry greater stigma and entail more restrictive placements—emotionally disturbed and mild mental retardation—have disproportionately been the preserve of students of color, while White special education students have disproportionately been classified as having learning disabilities (Artiles & Trent, 1994). In the late 1960s and throughout the 1970s and early 1980s, successful lawsuits emphasized the discriminatory treatment of overrepresented Latino and African American students in racially isolated special education classes. Because minority students have been segregated between special education classifications and in charter school enrollments (see Cobb & Glass, 1999; Howe & Eisenhart, 2000), the practice of steering most likely places, and will continue to place, a disproportionate burden on students of color with disabilities.

Because choice mechanisms often drive stratification by race, special education status, and other factors (e.g., among English-language learners), they present problems for those attempting evaluative comparisons. The steering associated with school choice results in the sorting of special education students disproportionately into traditional schools or choice schools geared toward such students. Therefore, test score comparisons between choice and traditional schools are likely to yield results driven overwhelmingly by these enrollment disparities. Policymakers and the public could be easily misled by simple contrasts that fail to account for these important differences in the students served by each type of school.

## POLICY INCENTIVES FOR STEERING AWAY SPECIAL NEEDS STUDENTS

Many choice schools are grounded in a market model; their survival depends on their ability to attract clients (students) who further the schools' aims of promoting the economic and educational success of its students. As such, there are incentives to steer away students who might hinder the schools' attracting the "right" kinds of students. These incentives include finances, accountability, and homogenization.

### Finances

Budgetary considerations drive perhaps the most powerful incentives for choice schools to steer away special education students. Special education students, particularly those with severe (so-called low-prevalence) disabilities, are extraordinarily expensive. Arsen and colleagues (1999) found "strong circumstantial evidence" of choice schools selecting students who cost less to educate (p. 75). They quote a founder of a small charter school: "'If a severely handicapped student enrolls in our school, we'll have to close'" (p. 76). Similarly, McKinney (1996) quotes an Arizona charter school principal: "'One severely disabled special ed kid would put me out of business'" (p. 25). Because of budgetary pressures, McKinney (1996) observes, "The marketplace concept that drives charter school legislation is stood on its head and proves to be a disincentive when it comes to serving children with disabilities."

## Accountability

Competition among public schools takes place within the context of high-stakes testing. State standards and accountability systems tie school finances, prestige, or both to students' test scores. Mean test scores rise and fall primarily with the entering test scores of students and only secondarily with the schooling these students subsequently receive (see Howe & Eisenhart, 2000). A choice school that recruits high-scoring students often gains the benefit of a state-run apparatus that financially rewards that recruitment and publicizes the test scores as demonstrating instructional excellence. Significant sanctions exist for choice schools that enroll students with low test scores, including the potential to lose their charter schools status.

## Homogenization

Operating along with these competitive and accountability forces is a choice school's desire to reflect a theme or a community vision. To a great extent, a choice school's success depends on being able to populate the community with children who further (or are at least not inconsistent with) that theme and vision. An aviation-themed magnet, for example, would clearly benefit from enrolling students with interests in, and knowledge about, aviation. The community and theme of a choice school, however while perhaps carefully designed in the formation stage, is built only partially upon that design and upon the hiring of faculty.

Charter school personnel often speak of these matters in terms of the "fit" between the student and the school (Arsen et al., 1999; Howe & Eisenhart, 2000; McLaughlin et al., 1996). In the case of a poor fit, according to school directors interviewed, school officials and parents will sometimes make a "mutual decision to withdraw the student" (McLaughlin et al., 1996, p. 5). Arsen and colleagues (1999), describing how "exclusion may take place either before or after students are enrolled in a particular school," explain that preapplications and interviews before enrollment make "it at least possible for administrators to discourage applications from students who might disrupt the school community" (p. 75).

In a related vein, McLaughlin and colleagues (1996) described how "more than one charter school representative voiced concern regarding the 'influence of the student population on the ability to maintain the focus of the school'" (p. 5). They related the story of a director of a charter school with "a very structured and highly academic curriculum" who, "in response to increased demand by parents of students experiencing learning problems for school admission, . . . asked the local district administrators for permission to apply selective admission criteria" (p. 8). The director expressed "concern that the parents of highly able students, who founded the school, may begin to withdraw their children" (p. 8).

## The Means of Steering

As mentioned earlier, steering away generally takes the form of claims by choice school representatives that they lack the necessary resources and facilities to meet the needs of children with disabilities or that these students are "unsuitable" for a given type or pace of curriculum. The Boulder, Colorado choice system, for example, requires that a special needs student must, after receiving "conditional acceptance" for enrollment at a school, "have a staffing which finds that the open enrollment placement is appropriate before a change in attendance can occur." This provides a formal means of steering special needs students away. It also provides an incentive for parents of special needs students to attempt to remove their children from special education. As reported by both a middle school principal and the parent of a special education student, these parents' perception is that their children will likely not be admitted to academically oriented choice schools because being special education allows them to be flagged and then denied via the "staffing" procedure.

Steering can take place preenrollment, during enrollment, or postenrollment and can take a variety of forms (Mulholland, 1999; Good & Braden, 2000). Sometimes, the approach is surprisingly direct. McKinney (1996) quoted the principal of an Arizona Montessori charter school: "We tell parents that the public schools provide the special education. We can't be set up for everything" (p. 22). Likewise, a choice official explained to McKinney and Mead (1996) why special education students are not allowed to participate in the choice plan: "We seldom permit children who require resource rooms to switch to other schools because the rooms are all alike" (p. 127). That is, the aspects of choice that make it appealing and worthwhile are not reflected in the services provided to these special education kids, so why should they participate?

Zollers and Ramathan (1998) found in Massachusetts that for-profit charter school operators told parents of special needs students that they were better off in traditional public schools. One administrator, for instance, told these authors, "We don't use IEPs; we tell parents that you have the option of a learning plan. Every kid has one" (p. 299). These learning plans or "learning contracts" lack the procedural safeguards or rights attached to an IEP. They are nonbinding on the schools (p. 299).

School officials are not the only choice school representatives who engage in steering away special education students. Many choice schools give a powerful role to parents. In Howe and Eisenhart's (2000) study of school choice in Boulder, a parent of a special needs student described her dealings with a choice school's parents: "I . . . talked to the parents and they laid it out. 'We're an aggressive school. We want the best test scores. The families are very driven; we want all the higher achieving kids.'"

Steering away, then, come in the form of discouragement or refusal to enroll. Alternatively, school officials can counsel the parent of a child with disabilities that the school does not fit their child. There can also be difficult application procedures, requiring such unnecessarily burdensome items as in-person interviews or meetings (Howe & Eisenhart, 2000). Another type of steering that appears to be fairly widespread concerns so-called sweat equity contracts. McLaughlin and colleagues (1996) note the "frequent requirement" of charter schools "for parents to volunteer a certain number of hours each semester" (p. 5). Parents who are too busy are sometimes allowed to buy out their time obligation, donating money targeted to hiring someone else to put in the time (see Howe & Eisenhart, 2000). These practices clearly favor parents with discretionary time and money.

For those students who are already enrolled but who present behavioral problems, steering may involve repeated suspensions. Zollers and Ramathan (1998) described this practice in for-profit charter schools in Massachusetts. One of the schools they studied, Boston Renaissance Charter School, was the subject of a decision of the Office of Civil Rights (OCR), in response to a complaint filed by the parents of a student with a disability, alleging violations of Section 504 (26 IDELR 889; OCR, 1997). The student was enrolled in kindergarten at the charter school and exhibited behavior difficulties. OCR concluded that the charter had violated the student's rights by failing to do the following: (a) provide the parents with notice of the procedural protections afforded them by Section 504, (b) provide supplementary aids and services and a continuum of special education services, and (c) permit the student to attend a full day of school.

In each of these instances of steering, school officials can be seen as responding to powerful budgetary, accountability, and homogenization pressures faced by most, if not all, choice schools. However, it may not be fair to conclude that these officials were intentionally violating disability law. Several researchers have also found a surprising level of ignorance concerning choice schools' responsibilities vis-à-vis students with disabilities (Lange, 1997).

According to a Colorado Department of Education official, charter schools in that state began realizing the extent of their special education responsibilities only once parents began complaining to the state, to school districts, and to the OCR (Charter schools and special ed law, 1996, p. 11). McKinney (1996), examining Arizona charter schools, tells of a free workshop for charter school personnel hosted by the state's Exceptional Student Services. The workshop was organized "in response to complaints by parents of students with disabilities who were told by charter principals to look elsewhere." Only 10 people attended the workshop, and, according to a state official, the "charter school representatives who did attend spoke in a single voice: 'Do I really have to do this?'" (p. 24). McKinney also reports that he examined Arizona charter school contracts and "found in almost all cases the state boards were approving charters without knowing how the school would provide special education" (p. 24). The breakdown, therefore, began much earlier in the process.

Yet in the face of considerable evidence on steering, Vanourek and colleagues (1997) respond, "Our own sense is that at least as much 'counseling' is happening in the opposite direction." But even if their hunch is correct, it misses an important point. The two opposing phenomena would be occurring in separate schools: Some charters would be actively recruiting these students and some would be actively avoiding them. In the process, the goal of inclusion would be lost.

### Policy Implications

IDEA's regulations provide that a child's placement is based on his or her needs, not on the ability of the school to meet those needs. The "needs" provision of IDEA is intended to protect the child from inappropriate placement. It should not be used to protect schools from placements that it finds undesirable. An Arizona charter school administrator, discussing his response to a parent of special education students, said, "We told her that her children wouldn't benefit from our program—you see, our Arizona law on special education says that children must benefit from special education—that makes a big difference" (McKinney, 1996, p. 24–25). This is an example of a charter school's using such a provision as an excuse—as a barrier to equal educational opportunities. It does not protect the child; it discriminates against her.

Even if a particular choice school is a poor match with the student's IEP, the school must take reasonable steps to provide a FAPE. "An amorphous recommendation by school personnel that a traditional public school could better serve the child would be clearly inappropriate" (Mc-

Kinney, 1998, pp. 570–571). But which steps do fall within the definition of *reasonable?*" Several states' charter school laws specifically allow for academic enrollment criteria. Earlier, we offered Heubert's (1997) opinion that academic schools could exclude special education students with inadequate test scores. Modifying this test-score requirement would purportedly place an undue hardship on these schools or fundamentally alter the nature of their services. Test-based admission is at the core of these schools' programs.

Assuming that courts and regulatory authorities reach conclusions consistent with Heubert's prediction, thus creating this exemption from the requirement of nonexclusion, we foresee a dangerous slippery slope. There should be no justifiable basis whereby schools where admissions are based on tests have a special claim to the criterion of "undue hardship." Accordingly, many choice schools may claim undue hardship on other grounds. Montessori schools, for instance, are constructed around student-directed activities that arguably require a certain level of maturity and behavioral control. Might these Montessori schools therefore be entitled to screen out immature or ill-behaved children? If a test is the *sine qua non* of the "undue hardship" standard, these schools could certainly develop their own admissions tests. Likewise, Core Knowledge schools would have no problem developing such tests. For other choice schools, sweat-equity contracts may constitute a key facet of the overall instructional program. Sweat-equity contracts are written parent-participation agreements to do work at the school for a certain number of hours. Failure to uphold the contract could result in students being asked to leave the school. For example, sweat-equity contracts are a feature of one of Boulder's charter schools, which is a member of William Glasser's Quality School Consortium. All these types of schools would likely place disproportionate limitations on students with disabilities, but they would seem to fall under the same type of exemption for undue hardship as do the test-based admission criteria of other schools.

We anticipate that the creators of choice schools—responding to the competition, accountability, and homogenization incentives—will design schools specifically to take advantage of the loopholes. Indeed, some already have. The "undue hardship" and "fundamental alteration" provisions then would become a tool to be abused by aggressive choice schools. We are not optimistic that OCR and the courts can or will do much to prevent such abuses within a legal/regulatory framework that isolates individual schools from larger educational systems.

Nor is it an easy matter for state enforcement officials to monitor and regulate the steering practices of charter schools. Clear procedures and guidelines are needed to allow for exemptions to protect innocent schools, but these rules also must ensure that students with disabilities are not routinely excluded. Such procedures and guidelines are likely to be effective only if they are crafted to apply at the state and district levels rather than piecemeal, at the level of individual schools. This is by no means a new insight; it was recognized in the drafting of those charter laws that we would call "equity driven/experimentalist" (and that proponents of a market approach call "weak," e.g., Center for Educational Reform). These laws require charter schools to hammer out agreements with local school districts in order to take the larger harms-benefits issue into account. Colorado is an example.

Colorado's original charter law (enacted in 1993) emphasized serving at-risk students, innovation, and dissemination of success. It provided that a school district's decision of whether to approve a proposed charter school could take into account whether a proposed charter school provided something not already provided by district schools. The district could also consider the harms and benefits of a proposed charter school to the district overall. In addition, the law included a statewide cap on charter schools of 100.

The basic rationale for the legislation was that freeing a limited number of schools to experiment might broadly improve the state educational system. But this rationale was always in tension with the market rationale, and the latter appears to be winning out (see Howe & Welner, 2002). Colorado also provides a case in point of how an equity-minded/ experimentalist rationale that takes into account the overall effects of charter schools can be subverted.

The original Colorado charter law, as well as the 1997 revised law, provided that founders of proposed charter schools who could not come to terms with local school districts, and were therefore denied a charter, could appeal the decision to the state board of education. The state board soon exhibited a strong penchant to side with charter school founders. After some initial resistance by local districts, one case went to the Colorado supreme court (*Board of Education v. Booth*, 1999). The supreme court ruled that the state board of education was legally authorized to order a local district to negotiate with a charter school applicant. In the wake of this court action, school districts have offered less resistance to the formation of charter schools. The response of the Boulder Valley School District was to permit the formation of a number of "focus" (basically magnet) schools and "strands" (basically choice schools within neighborhood schools, all of which were Core Knowledge). These schools have functioned along with several charter schools, with one result being the exacerbation of stratification by race, income, and special needs (Howe & Eisenhart, 2000).

The emphasis on serving at-risk students, and the innovation and dissemination tied to experimentalism, went by the boards as the advocates of the market rationale gained greater power. Consequently, Colorado's charter schools tend to emphasize academics, particularly core knowledge, and to underserve special education students. Along the way, the legislature amended Colorado's charter school law to remove the cap, also inserting language more congenial to academically oriented charter schools, thus putting its stamp of approval on the mix and character of Colorado's existing charter schools and encouraging more of the same (see C.R.S. §§ 22–30.5–101, *et seq.*, as amended in 1997).

Working in tandem with the charter law, and exacerbating pressures to steer away special education students, the Colorado legislature passed a stiff, high-stakes accountability law (Senate Bill 186, 2000; see, e.g., C.R.S. §§ 22–7–104, *et seq.*, §§ 22–7–601, *et seq.*, and §§ 22–30.5–301, *et seq.*, 2000) that mandates school report cards based almost exclusively on test scores. Disputes continue about whether and what kind of special education students might be excluded from the testing. Of course, if there are few or no special education students enrolled in a school, the question of whether some, and (if so) which ones, may be excluded from testing is a nonissue.

An effective policy response to the problem of steering special education students away from choice schools has two elements: (a) formulating and enforcing laws that incorporate an equity-driven/experimentalist rationale, including a restrictive cap, and (b) formulating and enforcing clear guidelines for determining undue hardship in the provision of a FAPE for special education students. Models for the former already exist. Models of the latter await development, but with the benefit of hindsight.

## CONCLUSION

The practice of steering special education students must be seen in terms of a much larger and highly complex set of problems that attend the growth of school choice. Notwithstanding this size and complexity, the root of the problem is simple, growing out of a fundamental clash between two mechanisms for distributing public education: the market versus democratic deliberation (Chubb & Moe, 1990).

The implementation of market-driven school choice has resulted in steering minority, low-income, and special education students away from certain choice schools, particularly ones stressing high academic achievement. It has also fundamentally altered the character of public deliberation about how to distribute education. Indeed, *public* deliberation seems to be disappearing. Such engagement requires accepting the inevitable trade-offs and compromises that have to be made in order for a public education system to best serve the interests of all students. By contrast, the market model enables parents—at least those with the savvy and necessary resources—to avoid "disharmony and conflict" and to simply shop around when they perceive their individual interests to be ill served by compromise. The exclusion of students who might reduce choice schools' "performance" is the predictable—if not inevitable—result of dispensing with public deliberation in favor of market solutions.

## NOTE

Dr. Welner's research for and preparation of this chapter were funded through the support of a postdoctoral fellowship granted by the Spencer Foundation and the National Academy of Education. Dr. Howe thanks the Boulder Valley School District and the Spencer Foundation for their financial support for the research upon which his BVSD research was based.

# Chapter 7

# Single-Sex Public Schooling as a New Form of Choice

## Implications for Diversity

AMANDA DATNOW, LEA HUBBARD,
and ELISABETH WOODY

A plethora of reform agendas have emerged in response to calls for improvement of the American public education system. There are movements for nationally driven standards and increased accountability, for a common curriculum, for democratic schools that focus on improving equity, and for comprehensive school reform. There are also efforts to expand school choice within the public school system. Fueling the choice movement are conservative social and political arguments regarding the power of the free market to inspire educational innovation, improve achievement, increase accountability, and regain parental support for public schooling (Gewitz, Ball, & Bowe, 1995). Increased school choice has been pushed through various forms, including magnet schools, charter schools, and voucher programs (Chubb & Moe, 1990; Cookson, 1994; Wells, 1993).

Alongside these reform movements have been concerns about gender equity in schooling. Many studies over the past 25 years have documented gender bias against girls in coeducational classrooms (for reviews, see American Association of University Women [AAUW], 1992; 1998a). Girls receive less teacher attention than boys, feel less comfortable speaking out in class, and face threats of sexual harassment in school (Sadker & Sadker, 1994; AAUW Educational Foundation, 1993). Although the achievement gaps between boys and girls are closing in some areas, girls' achievement still lags behind that of boys in math and science and, most significantly, in computer science and technology majors and careers (AAUW, 1998a; 2000). There is also concern that gender-equity solutions have reached girls of different ethnic groups unequally. For example, Latinas perform less well than other racial and ethnic groups of girls in several key measures of educational achievement (Ginorio & Huston, 2001).

While gender equity has long been discussed in terms of remedies designed to raise girls' achievement, more recently some scholars have begun to ask, What about the boys? (Gurian, 1998; Pollack, 1998). Public discourse has centered on a "crisis" for boys, focusing on their lower reading and language test scores and higher rates of special education referrals as compared with girls (Kleinfeld, 1999), as well as boys' greater propensity to be involved in violent crimes (Gilbert & Gilbert, 1998). All boys are seen as at risk of these problems, but most notably boys of color. Increasing rates of dropout and higher rates of incarceration are particularly salient for African American boys and men (Leake & Leake, 1992). In sum, gender bias is now understood as affecting both girls and boys, as neither group is immune to societal pressures and expectations.

Over the past several years, public schools in at least 15 states have addressed concerns about the achievement of boys and girls through experiments with single-sex education. Most often, these experiments have been in the form of separate math or science classes for girls (Streitmatter, 1999). Other manifestations of public single-gender schooling include Afrocentric academies for boys in Detroit, Baltimore, and Milwaukee and the Young Women's Leadership schools in Harlem, New York, and in Chicago. Some of these experiments have been found in violation of Title IX and have been forced to close or become coeducational.

Significantly, however, in May 2002, the federal government revealed its intent to draft new regulations that would provide more flexibility for, encourage, and help support single-sex public schools. Because of the loosening of Title IX that these regulations are expected to provide, we might expect to see many more experiments single-sex schools in the public sector over the coming few years. Up to now, most instances of single-sex schooling have been in the private sector in the United States.

Why the interest in single-sex public schooling? Single-sex schools rest on what many see as conflicting research evidence (see Datnow &

Hubbard, 2002), and most studies have been conducted primarily in the private sector and therefore may not generalize to public schools (for a review, see Mael, 1998). Nevertheless, advocates point to studies of Catholic single-sex and coeducational schools that find academic achievement benefits for girls and low-income and minority boys attending single-sex schools (e.g., Riordan, 1990; Lee & Bryk, 1986). Girls who attend all-girls schools are more apt to adopt leadership roles and to become engaged in traditionally male-dominated subjects such as math and science and to show improvements in self-esteem (Moore, Piper, & Schaefer, 1993; Streitmatter, 1999). Research on gender in the 1980s (Gilligan, 1982; Belenky et al., 1986), arguing that women learn differently from men, has also helped to provide justification for all-female schooling.

All-boys classes or schools are now looked upon as ways to improve literacy achievement and discipline (Gilbert & Gilbert, 1998) and are said to improve character development (Hawley, 1993). Advocates of all-male Afrocentric academies in public schools argue that the presence of African American role models and a focus on multicultural curricula can be beneficial in developing leadership skills and improving achievement for African American boys (Hopkins, 1997). Proponents of single-sex education also argue that the separation of the sexes is the most effective way to manage classroom behavior, through eliminating distractions and peer pressures for both boys and girls (Pollard, 1998). Clearly, the reasons behind the recent establishment of single-sex schools are no longer simple; they represent efforts to address not only gender bias but also racial and cultural issues.

It is in this reform context that California began the Single Gender Academies pilot program in 1997. California became the first state to experiment with single-gender public education on a large scale. In this chapter we present findings from a 3-year case study of these single-gender academies (SGAs) in six districts in California. The California legislation uses the term *single gender*, yet one could argue that *single sex* is a more appropriate term to describe the separation of boys and girls. However, for the purposes of this chapter, we use the term *single gender*, to maintain consistency with the language of the California experiment, and occasionally use the term *single sex* to refer to prior research.

The purpose of the study was to assess the consequences of single-gender schooling in the public sector. A major goal was to examine the equity implications of the California experiment. We conducted more than 300 extensive interviews with educators, policymakers, and students and carried out school and classroom observations. It is the most comprehensive study of single-gender public schooling that has been conducted in the United States to date.

In this chapter, we describe the California SGAs experiment, arguing that it was a movement primarily aimed at increasing school choice and addressing the underachievement of low-income students and students of color in separate academies of their own. We discuss how and why students chose to attend SGAs and the consequences for equity.

## THE CALIFORNIA SINGLE-GENDER
## PUBLIC SCHOOLING EXPERIMENT

In the 1997–98 school year, California's (then) Governor Pete Wilson pushed for legislation that resulted in the opening of 12 single-gender public academies (6 for boys, 6 for girls) in six districts. In Wilson's 1996 State of the State address he argued that single-gender academies were a way to provide public school students more options, more choice, and better preparation for real-world opportunities (California Department of Education, 1997). Later, in a speech at one of the SGAs, Wilson stated: "Kids need options . . . and single gender academies will stimulate competition and give kids opportunities they currently do not have because they are trapped in their schools and they need another approach." Expanding school choice was the key motivation for Wilson. This goal is quite different from the motivating forces behind the single-gender public schooling experiments we discussed earlier.

When single-gender schooling was proposed, the political climate across the nation and in California in particular was ripe for the expansion of school choice. In the preceding few years, California voters had passed conservative anti-immigrant and anti–affirmative action legislation, and the University of California regents voted to restrict all affirmative actions that benefited the admission of minority students to their campuses. At the same time, the number of charter schools in California continued to grow, staving off calls for voucher programs for several years. The movements to introduce more parental choice into the public system signaled a belief that the remedy for the ills of public schools was to gear schooling toward the needs and wants of particular groups and to force schools to compete for students. Therefore, the single-gender schooling experiment, designed as an optional program, fit well into the mood of the state.

According to sources at the state level, Wilson initially presented a plan in which all-male academies were magnet schools for at-risk boys and all-female schools focused on math and science. His expectation was that sex separation would allow for the establishment of strong disciplinary climates for boys and more attention for girls in traditionally male-favored subjects. It appears that beliefs about gender, race, and the definition of public schooling influenced his vision for these new schools. His initial plan for the SGAs raised concerns among legal advisors and feminists alike. Wilson's attorneys pointed out that attending to perceived gender differences could violate constitutional law, specifically Title IX. Feminist groups who had long fought for integration and equality saw the separation of the genders as a move toward inequality.

Despite Wilson's initial vision for different types of academies for boys and girls, a review of the final legislation and interviews with policymakers at both the State Department of Education and the governor's office revealed that a major intent was to ensure equality of the boys and girls academies. The legislation stated that while SGAs would "tailor to the differing needs and learning styles of boys as a group and girls as a group, . . . if a particular program or curriculum is available to one gender, it shall also be available to those pupils in the other gender who would benefit from the particular program or curriculum" (California Education Code, Section 58520-58524). In other words, there must be "equal opportunities at both boys' and girls' academies." These equality provisions were important in ensuring equal access to this new school choice option. After all, the "primary goal" of the legislation was to "increase the diversity of California's public educational offering" (Education Code Section 58520-58524).

The legislation instructed the California superintendent of public instruction to award grants on a competitive basis to "10 applicant school districts for the establishment of one single gender academy for girls and one single gender academy for boys, in each of those selected school districts" at the middle or high school levels under the pilot program (Education Code Section 58520-58524). In other words, a district that opened a school for one gender must open a second school for the other. Moreover, both schools had to provide equivalent funding, facilities, staff, books, equipment, curriculum, and extracurricular activities, including sports. Finally, while a single-gender school could be located on the campus of another school, it had to be a complete school, not entail just a single-gender class or program. These legal guidelines reflected an effort to stem legal challenges against single-gender public schools.

The push for equal opportunity was apparent in the allocation of funds. California's law allowed the school districts to receive $500,000 to operate single-gender academies at the middle or high school levels. The grant was to be divided equally between a district's boys and girls academies. The funding was intended as a development grant to schools; they would be able to use the money as they wished, but the expectation was that after 2 years they would fully fund themselves through average daily attendance money. The SGAs would operate magnet schools pursuant to the California Education Code. The legislation gave the responsibility of oversight of the SGAs to the State Department of Education. The legislation assigned management of the program to the Office of Educational Options. This action was "the basis on which this is being offered in California," explained a staff member. No extra funding was provided by the legislation for the administration of these new schools.

Two experienced staff members at the California Department of Education were charged with writing the Request for Proposals (RFP) based on the legislation and, subsequently, reviewing the proposals that were submitted. Initially, 24 districts expressed interest in proposing SGAs. Disappointingly, according to one State Department of Education official, there were only eight school districts that submitted proposals for funding. The grant opportunity was apparently not well marketed. The timing of the grant application posed a problem for some potential applicants, as there were only 2 months between the release of the RFP and the proposal deadline. A state official said that administrators in some districts were also concerned about the legalities of single-gender public schooling, despite assurances from attorneys that the legislation met the standards of Title IX. Of those eight that submitted proposals, one district's proposal was rejected because its design was not appropriate, and a second district pulled out of the review process because of legal concerns. In the end, only six districts in California were funded to start SGAs. These districts were not particularly unusual in any way and represented a broad range in terms of demographics, district size, location, and prior success at obtaining grant funding.

## IMPLEMENTING SINGLE-GENDER PUBLIC SCHOOLS: WHY, HOW, AND FOR WHOM?

In our interviews with educators and community members, we asked why they had started SGAs. We were interested in finding out which students the educators were hoping to serve in the academies, what problems they were aiming to address, and how the design of the academies would help them meet their goals. We found that many administrators sought the $500,000 because of the resources and opportunities that it would provide for students who were not successful in their school systems. In other words, instead of seeing the SGAs as primarily an opportunity to address gender inequities (as one might predict), most educators saw the grant as a way to help address the more typical educational and social problems of low-achieving students. In most cases, these were low-income students, primarily those of color. This is perhaps not surprising when one considers that the legislation stated that the academies needed to be designed with the "unique educational needs" of their students in mind, pushing some to focus on specific "at risk" populations.

To be sure, all the educators sought to increase school choice and to decrease distractions among boys and girls, and many sought to improve students' self-esteem. However, none of the proposals showed evidence that the SGAs were designed to address systemic gender bias. Thus, while one might assume that funding for single-gender public schools would provoke genuine interest from educators who held a commitment to single-gender education and that there was a strong theory behind why they were doing it, in the majority of cases, the reality proved to be quite different.

Educators' purposefulness in applying for the monetary grant was evident from their comments. The principal of the SGAs in the Palm school district said, "Why do I go for the single gender? What's so great? It's a great opportunity. It's also money. I can do something. If you have a traditional school . . . you've got to get extra money." With the grant, she was able to purchase the technology for Web TV, which provided students with access to an on-line curriculum at home. A school administrator in charge of another district's academies explained: "My main interest? Honestly, the gender part of it wasn't huge. I didn't really think about gender bias and all those sorts of things." Instead, the academies were seen as a way to improve the achievement of low-income and minority students—an option for "incoming ninth grade student populations that have shown a high potential to attend college but have achieved only poor grades in middle school" (*Birch Single Gender Academies Proposal*, 1997, p. 2).

The preceding examples point to the power of money in motivating district or school administrators to start single-gender schooling in their communities. The single-gender funding was a chance to provide new opportunities for students. With the grant funding, educators planned to develop social and academic support structures to address the problems of their particular student populations, such as low achievement, truancy, poverty, violence, or geographic isolation. As a result, the students the academies attracted and the curricular plans, organizational arrangements, and special services differed somewhat from site to site. Common among them, however, was a wealth of resources not typically available in public schools.

For example, the educators in one district (Evergreen) that is located in an isolated rural area of the state wanted to broaden students' experiences and opportunities. They purchased vans to transport students to San Francisco and Sacramento and other places of cultural and historic interest. The grant also provided for reduced teacher-pupil ratios, computers, and much-needed lab equipment. Even in places where school funding was perhaps not as scarce, educators found that they could use the SGAs funding to lower class size (not just in the single-gender academies but effectively across the whole school) and purchase technology not formerly available to them. In sum, the funding allowed schools to provide a new educational option with increased academic supports and resources.

Two of the six districts, Pine and Oak, also saw the grant funding as a way to address the needs of boys and girls in their communities. However, these districts differed notably from the others in that they had prior experience with single-gender education, and thus the grant was not the initial motivator. Pine district had operated a school for at-risk boys for 2 years prior to the grant funding's becoming available. The school opened as a result of the superintendent's concern for boys of color in the community, whom she saw as lacking male role models and subject to involvement in violent crimes at a young age. The school was initially established as a safe haven for at-risk, very low-income boys, where they would be provided with "tough love," structure, mentoring from adult males, and basic skills. The SGAs funding led the district to expand its SGAs, opening them to girls as well as boys (as required by the legislation), and to enhance the social and academic support services it offered on site.

Notably, a middle school in the Oak district had piloted two single-gender classes for 60 boys and girls in the 2 years prior to the grant's becoming available. The impetus for these initial classes was concern about the low self-esteem of adolescent girls that was documented in *How Schools Shortchange Girls* (AAUW, 1992) and *Reviving Ophelia* (Pipher, 1994). A teacher explained, "The whole idea behind [the initial experiment], particularly for the girls, was to give them enough strength emotionally, socially, and intellectually so that they can hold their own . . . in mixed classes." However, instead of serving a randomly selected, heterogeneous group as in the past, the grant-funded single-gender academies would aim to serve underachieving students with small class sizes, two full-time counselors, and additional classroom resources. Here again, even in this district, the state grant became a vehicle for educating low-achieving students, in a shift from the district's original vision of improving gender equity.

In sum, well-intentioned educators, many of them responding to economic and social realities in their schools and communities, found ways to use single gender as a vehicle for meeting needs through this new school choice option. Most commonly, educators sought to address the pressing academic and social issues of the low-achieving students in their communities. The grant money allowed them to address these needs through reduced class sizes, teacher teaming, academic support programs, counseling, and increased technology. Not surprisingly, the vision, design, and target population of the various SGAs strongly influenced who enrolled when the academies opened, as we explain below.

## CHOOSING SINGLE-GENDER PUBLIC EDUCATION

While sociopolitical context is key to understanding the advent of single-gender schooling at the state level and in each community, it is in the implementation of the legislation that one can unravel the implications of this new form of school choice. We hypothesized that the organization and implementation of each SGA would influence who would choose to attend. Undoubtedly, the most important issue regarding school choice in general, and single-gender schools in particular, is who chooses and who loses (Fuller et al., 1996). Prior research has shown that because parental choice of schools is race and class informed, it is of limited relevance to low-income parents because most choose not to participate (Gewirtz et al., 1995). These parents often experience an absence of sufficient information about the educational options available to them (Fuller et al., 1996; Wells, 1993), and therefore schools of choice often serve middle-class families more effectively. As we will explain, the implications of choice and equity worked out quite differently with respect to the SGAs in most districts in California, and this was largely a feature of how the choice was constructed.

A major goal of California's single-gender public schooling legislation was that it would expand choice for students and parents. However, we found that while clearly offering a choice to students within the public sector—a choice that is typically reserved for students who can afford to attend private schools—several of the single-gender public schools in California were, by design, not open to everyone. In some schools, who was eligible and who was able to attend the SGAs became a matter that was decided by the district in the proposal of its school and its target population. A number of the California single-gender schools became a mechanism through which to educate low-achieving, low-income, at-risk youth. However, the matter of choice was very context specific, and we believe that it is important to tease out some of the subtleties that existed in each site. While there was some measure of choice within all the districts, the degree of choice varied from site to site and among students.

## Information, Recruitment, and Choice

In our examination of choice and equity issues, we addressed the following critical questions: Was the community as a whole aware that single-gender schooling was a choice available to it? How was information disseminated? If there was more interest than space available, how were decisions made regarding who attends? Importantly, did the choice of single-gender schooling ameliorate or perpetuate race, ethnic, and gender inequities? As with any expansion of school choice, the establishment of SGAs also challenges us to consider the implications of this choice for the remaining school community. That is, when some students choose single gender, does it enhance or constrain the education of those students in the coeducational public school option?

Student recruitment for the SGAs occurred through a variety of means. In almost all districts, the academies were advertised through flyers; through mailers to students' homes, to district administrators, and to social service agencies; through the media, or a combination of these. Some students found out about the option from teachers or administrators who personally informed them about it. In the case of Pine and Palm, some students found out about the schools from law enforcement officials or social service providers. In several districts, educators were offered a new choice of where to put students, but it was not a fully democratic choice for students and parents. Once targeted, the parents made the final decision for students to enroll, but they and their children were often strongly encouraged toward the choice.

An assumption of the legislation was that the parents would embrace the choice of single-gender public schools. Educators believed that it would be quite easy to recruit students. This was true in some communities, such as Evergreen. Largely because of the special resources that were provided (i.e., field trips, computers), two thirds of the entire middle school population in the district opted to attend the single-gender academies (SGAs), which meant that only one coeducational class of 30 students was left at the K–8 school. The academy option was equally popular among boys and girls. Operating close to its intended capacity, the academies enrolled 28 boys and 30 girls in 1997–98. While anyone who applied for the SGAs was accepted, there was speculation by one administrator that the students whose parents could not read English or understand what was being offered in the SGAs did not apply for admission. The students who attended the academies were almost all (88%)

White; only a few were Latino or Native American, whereas the district as a whole was approximately 53% White.

At Evergreen, the advent of the SGAs was the first instance of school choice that had ever existed in the district. By contrast, in the Cactus district, the SGAs were one of a variety of school choices open to the middle school students in the district. The choice of any school was dependent on space, and entrance into oversubscribed schools was based on a lottery. Other district options included regular middle schools or schools "with approaches varying from traditional, self-contained classrooms and departmentalization to multi-aged, project based learning" (Fact Sheet, Cactus School District, Single Gender Academies). Transportation was not provided to middle school students who wished to attend a school outside their attendance boundary.

As we discussed, the SGAs at Cactus were initially founded to help the principal find a way to address the special needs of a new population of students, but the proposal was worded such that that they would attract a broad range—virtually anyone who might benefit. The girls who enrolled were primarily high-achieving students (a number of whom were performing *above* the 90th percentile) who were seeking a distraction-free, girls-only environment. One girl stated that "this is an opportunity that's available. . . . And then I thought it would be neat, you know, try something new, just to see if it helped." The 50 seventh- and eighth-grade students in the girls academy were predominantly White and from upper-middle-class backgrounds and lived in the surrounding upscale neighborhood in which the school was located. The minority students, mostly Southeast Asian and Latino, were from neighboring areas. Some had transferred to the campus because of the SGA option. The girls academy earned a positive image in the community, and in the 2nd year there was a waiting list.

While the girls academy was full, the boys academy at Cactus was underenrolled. Unlike the girls at Cactus, the majority of the boys who enrolled in the 1st year were low achievers. The school staff classified the majority of the 36 seventh- and eighth-grade boys as having behavioral problems and designated 6 as resource students. Some were African American and from low-income families who lived outside the surrounding area. A teacher explained: "A few parents . . . thought of it as a place where they could put their son. Maybe a military school, maybe more of a disciplinary, to correct the problems they were having." In the 2nd year, the profile of the boys academy changed, as did the teachers. Five of the boys who had exhibited behavior problems were expelled and another four had been counseled out of the academy. In addition, a staff member reported that since the girls SGA had received positive media attention, boys from private schools had enrolled in the boys SGA. The principal also reported that the "boys are a stronger academic group than last year.... There are fewer ... resource students." The 2nd-year boys SGA more closely resembled that of the girls in achievement levels, ethnicity, and social class than did the 1st-year boys SGA, but there were still far fewer boys interested in the choice than there were girls.

While Cactus had difficulty with recruiting boys, Pine and Palm had difficulty with recruiting girls. This created problems for these districts, as the SGAs grant guidelines stated that districts needed to serve equal numbers of boys and girls. Palm had many boys who wanted to attend but had trouble with recruiting girls, because fewer girls have discipline and academic problems that would lead them into the alternative school system. Moreover, as one teacher explained, the SGA at Palm did not offer a child-care facility, so teenage mothers would be more likely to choose another alternative school, with parenting programs. Approximately 60 boys and 30 girls were enrolled in 1997–98, the majority of whom were Latino. In general, the student population was said to mirror those of other alternative schools in the county in terms of ethnicity and social-class background.

Pine had difficulty with recruiting girls for some of the same reasons (e.g., fewer girls with troublesome histories), but also because the boys academy had the reputation of being "the school for the bad kids." The principal reported that "a lot of women don't want their girls with boys who may be problems." Teachers and counselors from neighboring schools saw the SGAs at Pine as a dumping ground to which to send their most problem students, and in fact they were encouraged by the district to do so. In 1997–98, 90 boys and 50 girls enrolled at Pine. Both the boys and girls who attended were a diverse mix of Latinos, African Americans, and Pacific Islanders, all from low-income backgrounds.

The disparity in numbers of boys and girls was always a concern of Pine's director. In order to make the SGA more appealing to the parents of girls, the school launched a public relations campaign in order to attract girls with academic problems, not discipline problems. In an article in the local paper, a reporter wrote, "The girls' school will not be for students at risk of dropping out. Instead, the focus will be on math and science, subjects with which girls often struggle. This summer, teachers are studying math and science curriculum especially designed for girls." In spite of such seductive public relations, no teacher reported participating in this staff development, and no changes appeared to have been made to the math or science curriculum. In the end, it proved difficult to change the makeup of the students.

In other communities, educators struggled to recruit students of both genders, and this ultimately affected student choice. The timing of the opening of the academies (with the funding received only after the start of the school year) proved problematic for some schools, as it left insufficient time for advertising the single-gender option. As the principal of Oak explained, "Most kids were settled in school by the time we started. The parents didn't want to change." While the planned enrollment was 90 students per academy in Grades 6–8, both operated under capacity in 1997–97 with 67 girls and 46 boys enrolled. While the girls academy represented the school as a whole with its diverse racial mix of Asian, Latino, African American, Middle Eastern, and White students, the boys academy had a much greater representation of African American students than that of the school as a whole. According to the principal, there was a "suspiciously high" number of resource specialist students who were referred to the academies by classroom teachers who wanted them out of their rooms.

During the 2nd year, recruitment was a bit easier at Oak, as there was more time to plan. The principal at Oak explained: "We asked for teacher recommendations and also publicized during our registration programs and I think that helped. And then some people came from other parts of the city specifically for this." After reading about the school in the newspaper, some parents of girls who had formerly attended private schools came to the SGAs, explained one teacher: "This year . . . I have a couple of boys but more of the girls have come out of private school." While having a more even mix of students in terms of ethnicity and prior achievement, the academies were still operating below capacity in the 2nd year.

A similar situation of underenrollment occurred at Birch, where students were being recruited to start in the SGAs in January. Also, there were practical constraints in recruitment. First, as some students may have been enrolled in French 1 elsewhere for the first semester, they could not continue with French in the SGAs, as these only offered Spanish 1. Second, the SGAs were one of many special programs at the school and thus had to compete for students who may have already found their niche elsewhere. There were political problems as well: While guidance counselors and administrators at the 10 high schools in the district were sent information about the SGAs, they did not actively promote this choice, as they were worried that the transfer of their students into the SGAs would result in a loss of average daily attendance funds at their schools.

In the end, the academies at Birch had to take all willing participants, regardless of whether they fit the profile of "underachieving" but with high potential; the boys tended to be very low achieving (some not necessarily believed to exhibit college-going potential), whereas the girls were typically more average. The ethnic mix in the academies was mostly similar to that of the district as a whole, except that African American students were overrepresented, constituting 29% of the girls SGA and 25% of the boys SGA, versus approximately 7% for the school and district as a whole. Capacity of each academy was 25 ninth-grade students. In January 1998, there were 22 girls and 18 boys enrolled at the academy's opening; however, enrollment shrank by the spring. The following year, enrollment was also open to 10th graders, but the academies still operated below capacity. Student recruitment was a constant challenge.

It bears noting that there was some attrition from one year to the next in all academies. In some cases, this was according to the students' choice. In others, it was the educators' choice, as explained earlier with reference to Cactus. Schools were sometimes able to remove, push out, or counsel out students who they felt did not belong. In almost every school, we heard stories of students who were removed for disciplinary reasons, particularly boys. Some students were removed if they were not performing up to the academic or social expectations of the academies.

## WHAT ATTRACTED PARENTS AND STUDENTS TO THE SGAs?

Oftentimes, educators attempted to sell parents and students on the special resources. In many cases, parents and students were attracted by these resources, and to a lesser degree by the single-gender arrangement. At Palm, brochures and flyers highlighted technology and career skills and invited students to "actively participate in your own education!" The school's technology focus was a major draw for students, whose other option would be to enroll in a much less resource-rich coeducational alternative school. As one young woman remarked, "It makes people want to learn here . . . 'cause they teach us in an interesting way." Similarly, a teacher recalled that the parents in Evergreen were "jazzed about the opportunity for the kids." When asked why they enrolled in the SGAs, students most commonly said that their parents wanted them to try it, usually citing the opportunities to go on field trips and use computers. Similarly, at Birch, an administrator said: "I think also one of the draws for both sets of parents were the smaller class size and the increased attention."

Very few boys and girls admitted to choosing the academies because they were single sex. Rarely was the goal of gender empowerment in a single-sex setting mentioned, except among a few parents of girls at Cactus. However, numerous students and parents mentioned the goal of lessening distractions in class as being important to them. As one male student said, "Like I get talkative and start talking to them [girls], then I get caught by the teacher." The same was true for girls. One girl explained: "My mom she thought it would be a good idea 'cause she thinks I like boys too much. I'm boy crazy or whatever." In a few cases, parents believed that if they placed their children in the SGAs, the latter would be subjected to less teasing.

At Oak and at Birch in particular, several Muslim students chose the SGAs for religious reasons. Some students reported to us that the Muslim religion prohibits coeducation, particularly for girls, once students reach adolescence. In some cases, students told us that while boys might be allowed to attend coeducational schools, girls would be more likely to be homeschooled. As one boy at Oak reported, his parents made him join the SGA because "it's part of [his] religion." A girl at Birch explained: "Ever since I've grown, my parents feel that I should be separated from boys because they think it's not a good surrounding. I think it's not a good surrounding. You know the drugs and the sex." She might have been homeschooled if not for the SGA option.

Significantly, the majority of students, both boys and girls, mentioned their mothers as central in their decision to enroll in the SGAs, rarely mentioning both parents or just fathers. In most schools, we heard that girls asked their parents if they could attend, whereas boys were more likely to be forced to attend. Many girls looked favorably upon the opportunity to be in classes without boys, believing these environments would be more comfortable. A teacher at Birch explained: "The girls chose to be in . . . and their parents just kind of signed on. . . . The boys are in there, I think, because their parents want them to be there." At this school, there was more initial interest among the girls and their families. He also stated: "The girls' parents could say, well, we're going to do this and the girls would go along." However, some of the boys protested, saying, "I don't want to be with all boys, that's stupid, that's gay," according to an administrator.

In several districts, parents' choice of the SGAs was shaped in part by the other options available. At Oak, a few parents reportedly saw the academic reputation of the school as a whole as a draw, and less so the single-gender nature of the program. Often, such information was learned through informal networks. As one student said, "My mom's friend works for [the district] and . . . she said this is like the best school." One Chinese boy explained that he and his parents were not specifically interested in the single-gender aspect of the school, but he wouldn't have been able to attend the coeducational school, because there were already too many students of his ethnicity, and the district operated with racial balance requirements. The shaping of options worked out quite differently in Evergreen. Students who did not elect to attend the SGAs had the choice to stay in the one remaining coeducational class on campus with a teacher who was new to the district and was reported to be unprepared to teach. Moreover, because so many of the better students were choosing the single-gender setting, the coed class was left with the students who had more disciplinary problems. Consequently, we are forced to qualify the term *choice* at Evergreen, since the coed option had become undesirable.

## CONCLUSION

In conclusion, we found that in most cases the choice of single-gender public education was structured by educators in their design of the academies, the timing of the grant, the other available options, and the special resources the academies offered. The primary goal of the SGAs legislation was to increase the diversity of California's public educational offering. However, we found that choice was limited from the outset and was determined by districts in their target populations and goals for the academies. In most cases, districts designed their single-gender schools for "at risk" students who were actively recruited to join. With the exception of the girls who enrolled in the SGA at Cactus and the students who attended Evergreen, the academies served student populations that tended to be more at-risk, of color, or low achieving than those attending regular schooling options in their districts. In these cases, the academies became a place in which to put students who posed challenges to educators. While, indeed, students did need to choose to attend, they were often recruited by educators who thought the academies would solve some of their academic and social problems.

In a few instances, efficacious parents were attracted by the additional resources available in the academies and sought to enroll their students. In some cases, single-gender education was attractive to parents as a way to lessen distractions, but the additional resources offered by the academies were also very important to them. Overall, however, the public interest in the choice of single-gender public schooling was not as intense as policymakers might have thought, and some schools struggled to fill their classrooms. In this regard, the California SGAs may have been a policy in search of a movement, rather than a movement in search of a policy (Wells, 2000).

The goals of the SGAs legislation were to increase the diversity of public educational offerings and at the same time provide equal access. Our findings suggest that neither intention fully panned out and give us pause about whether single-gender schooling is a wise move in the public sector, particularly if pursued under the policy framework that existed in California. Undoubtedly, the single-gender pilot program was not an ideal test case of single-gender public education, because circumstances limited who had the opportunity to apply for the grant and how it was implemented. In addition, educators lacked a strong philosophy for doing single-gender schooling, unlike their often more ideologically committed private single-gender-school counterparts (Hubbard & Datnow, 2002).

The policy for single-gender public schooling in California could have better enabled the successful implementation of single-gender public education through expanding the time in which educators had to prepare applications and providing state-level support in the areas of staff, instructional, and curriculum development. Most important, all public schools that separate students by gender must be as vigilant to the risks that other types of schools have faced that separate by race or any other criteria. Segregation might lead to a safe or comfortable space for some populations, but they clearly create tensions for equity. Consideration needs to be given to why such programs are important for students, what is gained as a result of their implementation, and what students and their peers might lose from not attending a mainstream educational program together.

## NOTE

Portions of this chapter derive from Datnow, Hubbard, & Woody (2001) and Datnow, Hubbard, & Conchas (2001). The work reported herein was supported by grants from the Ford Foundation and the Spencer Foundation. However, any opinions expressed are the authors' own and do not represent the policies or positions of the funders. We wish to thank the participants of our study, who kindly invited us into their schools, districts, and state offices and who were very generous with their time. We are also greatly appreciative of Gilberto Conchas, Barbara McHugh, and Jennifer Madigan for their research assistance. Our sincere thanks to our advisory board members Patricia Gandara, Peter Hall, Pedro Noguera, and Amy Stuart Wells for their insights throughout the study.

# Chapter 8

# Are Choice, Diversity, Equity, and Excellence Possible?

## Early Evidence from Post-*Swann* Charlotte-Mecklenburg Schools, 2002–2004

### ROSLYN ARLIN MICKELSON

The U.S. Supreme Court's recognition of the value of diversity for education in *Grutter* (2003) comes not a moment too soon for advocates of inclusive, equitable, and excellent public schools. Until the *Grutter* decision, the federal judiciary's withdrawal from race-conscious remedies to discrimination left many observers deeply concerned about the future of equality of educational opportunity (Boger, 2003; Chermerinsky, 2003; Orfield & Eaton, 1996). There still are reasons to be concerned about diversity in public education. School systems operating under federal desegregation orders are being declared unitary, and resegregation is fast approaching pre-*Brown* (1954) levels. At the same time, across the United States educational leaders are embracing school choice as *the* school reform most likely to provide diversity, equity, and excellence in education for the greatest number of students while researchers examine various aspects of choice reforms (Fiske & Ladd, 2000; Godwin & Kemerer, 2002; Henig, 1996; Peterson & Hassel, 1998; Willie et al., 2002; Witte, 2000).

In this chapter I present evidence from the Charlotte-Mecklenburg Schools (CMS) three semesters after the U.S. Supreme Court lifted the landmark *Swann* (1971) decision, and CMS implemented a districtwide neighborhood-school-based Family Choice Plan. I report what happens to racial and socioeconomic diversity, equity in opportunities to learn, and academic excellence when a racially and socioeconomically diverse community replaces mandatory desegregation with a race-neutral parental choice plan. The unique history and context of CMS offers the opportunity to examine how, in practice—as opposed to theory—choice operates on the ground.

If, in fact, diversity is an organizational precondition for educational equity and excellence in a multiethnic, economically heterogeneous community, and if school choice enhances diversity, one can argue that choice is a reform that should be widely embraced. Conversely, if choice stimulates resegregation—and its sequel of racial and socioeconomic inequities in opportunities to learn—we must conclude that school choice is a potentially harmful and dangerous reform that may hurt many of the students it is designed to help.

I begin with a discussion of the relationship of school racial composition to equity and excellence in education. After a brief review of the history of desegregation and choice in CMS, I present findings on the demographic shifts in school racial and socioeconomic (SES) composition 2 years after the implementation of the choice plan. The findings are used to answer three core questions: In an ethnically and socioeconomically diverse community, can a race-neutral school choice plan deliver diversity? Can it deliver educational equity? And can it deliver academic excellence? The chapter concludes with a discussion of the implications of this case study for other school systems seeking to enhance diversity, educational equity, and academic excellence through school choice.

## SCHOOL RACIAL COMPOSITION, EDUCATIONAL EQUITY, AND ACADEMIC EXCELLENCE

Arguably, the most pervasive and harmful manifestation of inequalities of educational opportunity is *de facto* segregation and the race-linked inequities in opportunities to learn that invariably follow from it. Even though the Coleman Report (Coleman et al., 1966) found that academic outcomes were better for Blacks who attended desegregated schools, social scientists, civil rights advocates, educators, and parents still question the harm of segregation and the benefits of desegregation (Armor, Rossell, & Walberg, 2003; Bankston & Caldas, 2002). This is not a matter of splitting hairs. If diversity is inconsequential in and of itself, the racial composition of schools matters very little for educational outcomes. However, if school racial composition affects school outcomes, any policy that subverts it must be carefully scrutinized, if not avoided.

Mounting evidence shows the positive academic effects of desegregated learning environments (The amicus briefs filed in the University of Michigan's affirmative action case lay out why diversity is important. See http://www.umich.edu/~urel/admissions/legal/amicus.html). Grissmer, Flanagan, and Williamson (1998) concluded on the basis of comparisons of National Assessment of Educational Progress (NAEP) scores over several decades that the narrower race gap in the 1980s and the increases in academic achievement of Black students in some states and not in others were the result, in part, of desegregation. In their reviews of the empirical literature on diversity's effects on learning, a number of scholars (Braddock & Eitle, 2003; Hallinan, 1998; Hawley, 2002) independently conclude that students who learn in diverse schools are likely to gain an education superior to that of students who do not have this opportunity. My own survey research in Charlotte revealed that the longer CMS Blacks and Whites learned in racially balanced schools and classrooms, the better were their academic outcomes (Mickelson, 2001b, 2003).

How does school and classroom racial composition affect academic outcomes? Students in racially imbalanced schools (who tend to be Blacks, Latinos, and Native Americans) are more likely to have fewer material and teacher resources; a weaker academic press; and greater concentrations of poor, homeless, limited English-speaking, and immigrant students than students in racially balanced schools (Kahlenberg, 2001; Lee & Burkham, 2002; Natriello, McDill, & Pallas, 1990). Students in predominantly minority schools have access to fewer advanced-placement classes than students in majority White schools (Pachón et al., 2003). Although in this chapter I do not discuss classroom segregation (tracking, ability grouping), it is a significant source of educational inequality (see Lucas, 1999; Meier, Stewart, & England, 1989; Mickelson, 2001b; Oakes, Muir, & Joseph, 2000; Wells & Crain, 1994; Welner, 2001).

Human resources—such as high-quality, credentialed teachers instructing in their area of expertise in small classes (Darling-Hammond, 2000; Ingersoll, 1999; Lankford et al., 1995)—are directly related to school finances. Racially isolated schools and classrooms are less likely to have the best- qualified teachers. Other, less tangible human resources are indirectly related (through the racial and SES composition of communities) to a school's funding level, such as stable peers, active involvement of parents, motivated peers who value achievement and who share knowledge with classmates, and a school climate imbued with high expectations (Kahlenberg, 2001). Students who attend resource-poor schools are disproportionately members of minority groups (Duncan & Brooks-Gunn, 1997; Lee & Burkam, 2002; Payne & Biddle, 1999). Given the system of public school financing, which is largely dependent on property taxes (and in view of the racial segregation in public and private housing markets [Powell (*sic*)] et al., 2001), it is not surprising that there are striking race (and class) differences in school revenues and related opportunities to learn. Whether money matters for school outcomes is a long-standing debate dating back at least to the Coleman Report's finding that funding is not closely related to achievement (Coleman et al., 1966). Although skeptics remain unconvinced (Hanushek, 1997), a growing body of research establishes that money *does* matter and that where and how the money is spent is also extremely important (Ferguson, 1998a, 1998b; Greenwald, Hedges, & Laine, 1994; Hedges, Laine, & Greenwald, 1994).

## HISTORY OF DESEGREGATION IN CMS

The historical significance of CMS rests on its legacy as the first district to use mandatory crosstown busing, to express racial goals for student assignments to schools, to set forth faculty and staff ratios at each school, and to pair schools in racially distinct neighborhoods as remedies to segregation (Boger, 2002, 1; *Swann*, 1971, pp. 22–31). From roughly 1974 to 1992, CMS employed mandatory busing to achieve a racial balance of approximately 40% Black and 60% White and other students in each of its schools (Douglas, 1995; Smith, 2004). The target ratio of 40% Black to 60% White/other is based on the district's racial composition at the time of the *Swann* ruling (25% Black plus a ±15% margin). As the district's Black population grew, so did the criterion for racially balanced schools.

CMS is unique in other important respects. Until 2002, it was a majority White district. In 2003 the district became approximately 6% Asian and other ethnic groups, 43% Black, 8% Hispanic, and 43% White. These demographics mean that school and classroom diversity is feasible. The district is a countywide system encompassing 530 square miles. By North Carolina law, students are bused to school if they live more than 1 mile from their school; consequently, the majority of busing miles has been for transportation rather than desegregation. Since the implementation of the choice plan, overall busing has increased in terms of numbers of students, miles, buses used, personnel, and costs. As in many countywide school systems, income and wealth in CMS vary widely. It is a both urban and suburban system, with poorer people concentrated in the central portion of the county.

Although the city's desegregated schools were once a source of civic pride (Mickelson & Ray, 1994), the broad social and political coalition supporting desegregation began to crumble in the late 1980s. The coalition's demise was an unintended consequence of the chamber of commerce's successful campaign luring firms to the area. Relocating top management and professional found the schools in Charlotte-Mecklenburg desegregated not only by race but also by social class. In the early 1990s, a middle-class Black mother told me, "If I wanted to send my children to school with students from the projects or the trailer parks I would have moved next to one."

Further, parents encountered a school system struggling to overcome the legacy of decades of underfunded public education, a legacy that often led to a conflation of the results of funding deficits with the results of desegregation. By the late 1980s, discontented suburban newcomers and civic and business leaders began to pressure the schools to end busing for desegregation (Mickelson & Ray, 1994).

Most of the mandatory busing plan was replaced by other desegregation strategies in 1992. Most notable was a program of controlled choice among magnet schools (CMS, 1992). The 1992 controlled choice magnet plan was adopted as a means of voluntary desegregation. Consequently, applicants in the magnet school lottery were placed on two lists, one for Blacks and one for Whites and other ethnic groups. This use of racial guidelines for magnet school admissions eventually became the ostensible basis for a lawsuit by White families seeking to end CMS's use of race-conscious policies of any kind.

In 1997 William Capacchione, claiming the race-conscious magnet lottery violated his daughter Christina's 14th Amendment rights to equal protection, sued CMS, seeking a declaration of unitary status, an end to mandatory desegregation, and an end to any current and future race-conscious policies (*Capacchione et al. v. Charlotte-Mecklenburg Board of Education, 1999*). Shortly after the Capacchione family filed its lawsuit, the original Black plaintiffs, perceiving the lawsuit as a threat to the *Swann* ruling, intervened by reactivating their original case against CMS. Two young Black families with children currently enrolled in CMS, the Belk and the Collins families, joined the *Swann* plaintiffs. Because the two lawsuits mirrored each other—the White plaintiffs requesting a declaration of unitary status and the Black plaintiffs requesting a thorough implementation of the original *Swann* order to desegregate—the judge consolidated the two cases (*Swann sub nom Belk* and *Capacchione*) into one. Although the trial judge, Robert Potter, had been a citizen activist "unequivocally opposed" to mandatory busing for desegregation before President Ronald Reagan appointed him to the federal bench (Morrill, 1999), he did not recuse himself.

In September 1999, the trial judge declared CMS unitary (*Capacchione*, 1999). He enjoined CMS from using race in any future operations of the school system and awarded the White plaintiffs attorneys' fees and nominal monetary compensation for damages to their constitutional rights suffered under the school system's use of the race-conscious magnet lottery.

A three-judge panel of the Fourth Circuit Court of Appeals overturned the lower court's unitary decision in November 2000. Almost a year later, the full appellate court, sitting *en banc*, reversed its three-judge panel and affirmed the lower court's 1999 unitary decision. But the full court's majority agreed that the race-conscious magnet plan was not unconstitutional (Capacchione's original complaint), and absent a constitutional violation, the White plaintiffs were not entitled to attorneys' fees or damages. Both plaintiffs appealed to the U.S. Supreme Court. CMS became unitary when the Supreme Court denied the Black plaintiffs' *certiorari* petition on the issue of unitary status (*Belk*, 2002), and the White plaintiffs' *certiorari* petition regarding the issue of attorneys' fees (*Capacchione*, 2002). It is important to note that the courts recognize that the schools in Charlotte-Mecklenburg are becoming increasingly racially identifiable. To paraphrase Hochschild and Scovronik (2003, p. 51), courts may deem that a school system segregated by (legal) practice rather than (illegal) mandate is constitutional.

## CMS'S CHOICE PLAN

Even though CMS continued to operate under *Swann* during 2001, the majority of the school board believed that the Supreme Court ultimately would uphold the lower courts' decision declaring CMS unitary. Fully a year before the Supreme Court upheld Potter's 1999 unitary decision, on April 3, 2001, CMS adopted a neighborhood-school-based choice plan in preparation for the 2002–3 school year (CMS, 2001a).

The Family Choice Student assignment plan divided the 530- square mile countywide school system into four geographic zones designed to maximize a balance of race, ethnicity, income, and population density. The plan's key features include (a) stability of school assignments over a student's educational career in CMS, (b) a guaranteed school assignment near the family's home if that school is the one parents choose, (c) guaranteed options to choose enrollment low-poverty/high-performance schools for students in schools with extremely high concentrations of student poverty (as long as seats are available in the low-poverty/high-performance schools) (Taylor, 2003), (d) magnet school choices among a variety of themes, and (e) maximum utilization of all schools' seat capacities.

The majority of the school board also anticipated that absent a race-conscious component to the magnet lottery, the new neighborhood-schools-based choice plan would unleash powerful social, psychological, and economic forces that would lead to resegregation and gross inequities in opportunities to learn. In fact, the school board's chairperson cast the lone dissenting vote against adoption of the choice plan precisely for this reason. In another resolution adopted in July 2001, the board pledged to ensure equity across all schools (CMS, 2001b, 2001c). The deliberations of the board indicate that all members were aware that the plan was likely to resegregate the district by race, socioeconomic status, and performance. The school board and the superintendent were also well aware that concentrating poor, low-performing, and otherwise at-risk students into schools makes it more difficult and more expensive to teach them successfully. CMS's own consultant, Professor Gary Natriello (Natriello, 1999; Natriello, McDill, & Pallas, 1990) told the school board, the superintendent, and the community as much when he publicly testified about these matters at a school board meeting in the fall of 1999.

A major equity component of the Family Choice Plan is the *choice-out* option. As it is designed, starting in the 2003–4 school year, students assigned to home schools that have at least 30% more than the district's average concentration of low-income students can move to the top of the list for admission to schools with below-average poverty if there are seats available (Helms, 2003b). Intended to address issues of high concentrations of poor and low-performing students, this choice-out option is central to the equity compromise that permitted the school board's majority to adopt the Family Choice Plan.

To participate in the Family Choice Plan, parents are required to fill out a choice application and to select three schools within one of four geographic areas into which the county is divided. Even if a family expects to attend its neighborhood school, parents must designate it as the first choice. Families are guaranteed their "home" school if that is their choice, and families may choose another school within their zone, and receive free public transportation to it. If they are admitted to a magnet school outside their zone, students do not receive free public transportation. In the fall of 2002, CMS began to operate its Family Choice Plan.

## METHODS AND DATA

The data presented in this chapter are part of my 15-year multimethod case study of school reform in CMS. CMS itself is the primary source of the data I use in this chapter. CMS publishes enrollment data by student race and eligibility for free or reduced-price lunch (the district's measure of SES) for each school. I compared 2001–2 (before choice) student demographics by school with those from 2002–3 (after year 1 of the choice program), and fall 2003–4 (after year 2) demographics with those from 2001 (before choice). These comparisons enabled me to determine if the racial and socioeconomic demographics of schools changed after the implementation of the choice plain, and if so, in which directions.

To a lesser extent, I use the results of surveys of CMS high school and middle school students that I conducted in 1997. In that year, most students who took my survey spent much if not all of their CMS educations in desegregated schools. A portion of the respondents spent some or all of their educations in segregated Black schools. And all the students experienced within-school segregation throughout secondary school, because CMS employs extensive tracking in all math, science, social studies, and English courses. These survey data enabled me to examine the effects of school and classroom racial composition on both opportunities to learn and achievement. The data also allowed me to examine the relationships of family background (parental educational and occupational attainment, cultural capital), student characteristics (race, gender, prior achievement, effort, attitudes toward education, peer group), and school organizational factors to academic outcomes (grades and test scores). The details of my methodology, the survey instruments, the analyses, and overall findings from these surveys have been published elsewhere (Mickelson, 2001a, 2001b, 2003). In this chapter, I refer only to the major findings from these surveys. A third source of data are published media reports, CMS reports and archival records, and interviews I have conducted with school personnel, parents, and civic leaders.

## FINDINGS

### The Effects of Desegregation on 1997 Achievement in CMS

Using my 1997 data sets, I examined the effects of cumulative exposure to segregation and desegregation on achievement over the course of a student's educational career in CMS. I compared the effects of school and classroom racial composition on North Carolina end-of-grade (EOG) and end-of-course (EOC) test scores while controlling for individual-, family-, and school-level covariates of achievement. I reached three main conclusions: First, students—both Black and White—who have experienced desegregated schools and classrooms have benefited academically in significant and substantive ways. Second, racially identifiable Black schools *and* classrooms exert significant negative effects on both Black and White students' academic outcomes. Third, even in desegregated middle and high schools, tracking (within-school resegregation) helps to maintain White privilege by placing Whites disproportionately into higher tracks than those of their comparably able Black peers. This practice increases Whites' access to better teachers and other resources, while it diminishes access to superior opportunities to learn for students in racially identifiable Black tracks and schools (Mickelson, 2001a, 2001b).

As discussed earlier, CMS ended all desegregation efforts when it became unitary in April 2002. The previous year, the school board adopted both the Family Choice Plan for the 2002–3 school year and an equity resolution to help ensure that the transition from court-mandated desegregation to race-neutral school choice did not unravel the equity and achievement gains of the past 31 years.

## Who Gets Their Choice?

In January 2002, parents of every student completed an application on which they indicated their first, second, and third choices of schools. During the plan's 1st year, the majority of families received their first, second, or third choices. Among families who did not, however, Blacks were the least likely to receive any of their first three choices. They were also the least likely ethnic group to name their neighborhood schools as one of those choices (Helms, 2002). In the 2nd year of the choice plan's operation, similar patterns obtained. Fewer families received their first three choices (Helms, 2003a, 2003b). Several factors account for this pattern: The inferior quality of schools in the central city compared with the caliber of those in the suburbs, recent suburban growth patterns in the county, and the school board's choice of school sites during the past 20 years set the stage for the inequities in families receiving their school choices. Furthermore, suburban parents opting for their neighborhood schools fill them to overcapacity. Overcapacity requires the school district to use mobile classrooms to accommodate "neighborhood" families while it forecloses suburban choices to those (primarily Blacks) who wish to attend the higher-performing schools. Adding to overcapacity problems is the fact that during the 1st year of the plan's operation, the school board frequently granted waivers to vocal, "involved" families, enabling their children to attend a school outside their choice zone (Simmons, 2004).

## Resegregation by Race and Social Class

The racial composition of many CMS schools shifted after implementation of the Family Choice Plan. Table 8.1 presents the changing demographics of CMS in the 1st and 2nd years of postunitary status. An examination of the shifts between the 2001–2 and the 2003–4 school years suggests a rapid pace of resegregation in the district under the choice plan. As a difference between the 2001–2 and the 2003–4 school years, 21.4% fewer elementary schools and 14.7% fewer high schools are racially balanced; 3.2% more elementary schools and 10.7% more high schools are racially identifiable Black; and 18.2% more elementary schools, 4.5% more middle schools, and 4% more high schools are racially identifiable White. Middle schools break the pattern of resegregation—3%

**Table 8.1.** CMS Postunitary Racial Demographics by School Level, 2001–2 through 2003–4 (Actual)

| | Elementary | | | Middle | | | High | | |
|---|---|---|---|---|---|---|---|---|---|
| | 2001–2 | 2002–3 | 2003–4 | 2001–2 | 2002–3 | 2003–4 | 2001–2 | 2002–3 | 2003–4 |
| N of Schools | 86 | 85** | 87 | 26 | 27 | 29 | 16 | 17 | 17 |
| % Racially Balanced* | 57 | 37.6 | 34.4 | 38.4 | 29.6 | 31 | 50 | 35.3 | 29.4 |
| (N) | (49) | (32) | (30) | (10) | (8) | (9) | (8) | (6) | (5) |
| *% Change 2001–3* | | -22.6 | | | -7.4 | | | -20.6 | |
| % Racially Identifiable Black | 29 | 37.6 | 38 | 38.4 | 37 | 41.4 | 18.7 | 29.4 | 35.3 |
| (N) | (25) | (32) | (33) | (10) | (10) | (12) | (3) | (5) | (6) |
| *% Change 2001–3* | | +9 | | | +3 | | | +16.6 | |
| % Racially Identifiable White | 14 | 24.7 | 25.6 | 23.1 | 33.3 | 27.6 | 31.3 | 35.3 | 35.3 |
| (N) | (12 ) | (21) | (24) | (6) | (9) | (8) | (5) | (6) | (6) |
| *% Change 2001–3* | | +11.6 | | | +4.5 | | | +4 | |

*Source:* Charlotte-Mecklenburg Schools Class Counts, May 2002; Charlotte-Mecklenburg Schools, Monthly Membership at End of Month One, September 17, 2002; September 18, 2003.

* Based on ± 15% CMS Black population for each year.

** The Ns change as old schools close for repair or replacement and new ones open.

more are racially balanced, while 7.4% fewer middle schools are racially identifiable Black in fall 2003—but 4.5% more are racially identifiable White.

The results of the 2003–4 lottery show that in the 80 CMS schools, student populations with the highest percentage of White students are also those with the lowest percentage of students on subsidized lunches. When the resegregation data in Table 8.1 are juxtaposed with these race/ poverty concentration data, we can see how current CMS pupil assignment policies create the organizational framework for racially correlated inequities in opportunities to learn.

The jump in resegregation in schools translates into an the increase in the proportion of Black students learning in segregated schools, a trend that began in the mid-1990s when the voluntary magnet plan replaced mandatory busing. From 1991 through 1994, roughly 19% of Black students attended racially imbalanced Black (RIB) schools. In 1996, the count rose to 23%, and by 2000, 29% of Black students attended RIB schools. In 2001, the number jumped to 37%. But in the 2002–3 school year, fully 48% of CMS Black students attended RIB schools (CMS, 1970–2002).

## Over- and Underutilization of School Facilities

The resegregation described in the previous paragraph also means that there are now significant imbalances in the utilization of school seating capacities. The conservative standards I use in calculating underutilization are intended to compensate for the intentionally lower classroom size in Equity Plus II schools.

Under- and overutilization patterns are related to the schools' racial composition. As Table 8.2 indicates, in the 2002–3 academic year, all but 1 of the 39 underutilized schools was a racially imbalanced minority school (here I calculated imbalance by summing Black and Hispanic students into one "minority" category). Of the 33 overutilized schools, 6 (3 elementary and 3 high schools) are minority, 13 are racially balanced, and 14 are racially identifiable White.

With two exceptions, underutilized schools also underperform on North Carolina's standardized tests (EOCs and EOGs). CMS designates chronically underperforming schools with high concentrations of low-income students and proportionately fewer qualified teachers (based on their licensure and experience) as Equity Plus II schools. These schools receive additional resources, including smaller classes and teacher bonuses (CMS, 2001b). Table 8.2 indicates that at every level, underutilized schools that are also Equity Plus II schools are racially isolated minority

**Table 8.2.** Utilization of Seat Capacity by School Level, Racial Composition of Student Population, and Equity Plus Status, CMS 2002–3.

Underutilization of Capacity

| Level | Elementary | | | Middle School | | | High School | | |
|---|---|---|---|---|---|---|---|---|---|
| Standard | <80% | | | <80% | | | <90% | | |
| Range | (52%–79%) | | | (57%–79%) | | | (76%–89%) | | |
| | RIM | RB | RIW | RIM | RB | RIW | RIM | RB | RIW |
| N | 25 | 1 | 0 | 8 | 0 | 0 | 5 | 0 | 0 |
| N Equity Plus II | 24 | 0 | 0 | 8 | 0 | 0 | 5 | 0 | 0 |

Overutilization of Capacity

| Level | Elementary | | | Middle School | | | High School | | |
|---|---|---|---|---|---|---|---|---|---|
| Standard | >100% | | | >100% | | | >100% | | |
| Range | (102%–139%) | | | (102%–111%) | | | (116%–131%) | | |
| | RIM | RB | RIW | RIM | RB | RIW | RIM | RB | RIW |
| N | 3 | 7 | 3 | 0 | 3 | 5 | 3 | 3 | 6 |
| N Equity Plus II | 0 | 0 | 0 | 0 | 0 | 0 | 0 | 0 | 0 |

*Source:* CMS, Monthly Reports, 2002a (September 17).

schools. Conversely, none of the overutilized schools, irrespective of their racial composition, is an Equity Plus II school.

There are several reasons for the relationship between underutilized schools and Equity Plus II status. Class size is smaller by design in Equity Plus II schools. Another reason is that parents tended not to choose low-performing neighborhood schools (Helms, 2002, Holme, 2002). The nexus of race, poverty, and low performance evident in underutilized Equity Plus II schools requires further study. However, early findings from CMS's choice plan suggest how race, SES, school quality, and choice intersect in ways that disadvantage poor children and children of color.

## Educational Equity

*Do Parents Utilize Their Choice-out Option?.* According to the equity compromise enacted when the school board adopted the Family

Choice Plan, parents of students attending schools with concentrated poverty 30% over the district's average may choose to transfer their children to a lower-poverty school. CMS expects parents to exercise this option during the January window when it accepts choice applications for the following school year.

During the 1st year of the Family Choice Plan the lowest-performing schools had the highest concentrations of poor and racial minority children. Low-income, undereducated, and non-English-speaking parents tend to be least likely to be involved in their children's education without outreach efforts from CMS. Yet CMS does not provide targeted information about choice-out options to parents of students who qualify. Moreover, given the overcrowding in the most desirable schools, parents of choice-out students are limited in regard to the schools to which they can transfer their children. Parents are not informed of which schools they may choose to transfer their children to in lieu of their high-poverty schools. Not surprisingly, near the end of the choice application period in January 2003, of the 9,600 students eligible for choice-out, only one parent had inquired about the program (see *Educate*, 1/23/03 p. 3).

*The Politics of School Equity.* In 2001, when the school board enacted both the Family School Choice Plan and the Equity Plan, Democrats held the majority of seats on the Mecklenburg County Commission. The commission's chair, a Democrat, was instrumental in forging the political concession that led to the school board's 8-to-1 vote to adopt the choice plan: If the school board adopted the Family Choice Plan in 1999, the county commission would fund the equity programs that the school board deemed necessary to provide all children the highest-quality education in the resegregating school system. But the board delayed adopting a pupil assignment plan until after the Supreme Court's decision in *Capacchione*, and the county commission may not have enough funds for equity policies.

The school board adopted the Family Choice Plan in April 2001 (CMS, 2001a) and the Equity policy in July 2001 (CMS, 2001b), and in the November 2001 election Democrats were swept from leadership on the Mecklenburg County Commission. The county commission's commitment to fund equity in the resegregating school system departed with the Democratic majority. Since then, CMS has not received the budgets that permit it to implement fully the promised equity programs (such as class-size reductions in Equity Plus II schools and expansion of prekindergarten). CMS cannot maintain prechoice funding levels for regular programs, because the county adopted a zero-increase school budget despite annual growth of 3 to 4% in the number of students, and many of the voter-approved new constructions and renovations of old schools—an integral component of the equity plan—have been delayed by the county commission because the recession of 2003 means fewer tax dollars are available overall for public services and tax increases will jeopardize the county's bond ratings.

## Academic Excellence

For better or for worse, the contemporary gold standard of academic excellence is standardized test scores (Hawley, 2002). Effects of the Family Choice Plan on CMS's 2002–3 test scores are not yet knowable. The reconstitution of schools' populations as a result of the choice plan means that school-level comparisons are impossible without individual-level growth scores. As of this writing, individual-student-level test data are not available. Moreover, the state of North Carolina renormed its EOG and EOC standardized tests during the 2002–3 academic year, making any comparisons of achievement before and after the implementation of the choice plan more difficult. Nevertheless, it is possible to report that 2002–3 school-level EOG and EOC test scores throughout CMS remain correlated with school racial and socioeconomic composition.

## DISCUSSION AND CONCLUSION

### Choice and CMS's Educational Perfect Storm

In the wake of CMS's neighborhood-schools-based choice plan, diversity and the potential for educational equity and academic excellence have been swept away by a "perfect storm" (Boger, 2003). Boger describes North Carolina education's perfect storm as the intersection of racial resegregation, high-stakes testing, and school resource inequities. Each force—segregation, testing, and resources—is a formidable challenge to professional educators. Boger observes that the convergence of the forces can overwhelm even seasoned professionals who tend to focus on individual threats rather than on their combined power. The specific version of education's perfect storm in CMS involves the convergence of the new choice plan's implementation with the population pressures from the successful chamber of commerce campaign to attract new firms to the community, the fiscal crisis at local and state levels, and the ascension to power of a Republican majority on the Mecklenburg County Commission. The union of these circumstances puts full funding for CMS's operating budget and equity plan into the hands of a fiscal authority guided by conservative ideological principles and priorities not necessarily sympathetic to public education in general, and CMS, in particular.

## Implications of the Charlotte Case

Within the first three semesters of operating under the Family Choice Plan, CMS violated several of its interrelated guiding principles: the guaranteed option to choose to enroll in a high-performing school for students in poor-performing schools, maximum utilization of all school facilities, and equity across all schools. CMS never promised that its choice plan would deliver greater diversity, and the district is, in fact, rapidly resegregating by race and social class. Given the mounting evidence that school and classroom diversity are integral to educational equity and academic excellence, these trends are troubling.

I now return to the three core questions raised earlier in the chapter: In an ethnically and socioeconomically diverse community, can a race-neutral school choice plan deliver diversity? Can it deliver educational equity? And can it deliver academic excellence? CMS's choice plan has triggered an acceleration of the nascent trend toward racial and socioeconomic segregation. Given the dynamics of residential segregation, its race-neutral neighborhood-schools-based choice plan cannot produce diverse schools. The funding of equity policies rests on the slender reeds of partisan politics and the tenuous public commitment to equity in education even in the best of economic times. The comprehensive failure of the choice-out option to realistically provide the promised equity safety-value for students in the least desirable schools foreshadows the unlikely success of No Child Left Behind's comparable provision. The academic consequences of choice in CMS remain to be seen, but given the harmful effects the policy has on student diversity and educational equity in opportunities to learn, it is unlikely that choice will be the educational-reform silver bullet its proponents expect.

There are unique circumstances that make it difficult to generalize from the outcomes described in this case study. Nevertheless, the findings are instructive, because unlike most prior studies of choice, the evidence presented in this chapter reports choice's *districtwide* effects on diversity, educational equity, and academic excellence, not just the effects on a subset of a district's students. The holistic, historical perspective of the case study means that even the early evidence presented in this chapter is useful beyond Mecklenburg County. CMS's experiences

with diversity, educational equity, and academic excellence since beginning its the Family Choice Plan make for a cautionary tale for other
school systems with similar goals.

## NOTE

The research reported in this chapter is supported by grants from the Ford
Foundation (985-1336 and 1000-1430) and from the National Science Foundation
(RED-9550763).

# Conclusion

## *Envisioning School Choice Options That Also Attend to Student Diversity*

### JANELLE T. SCOTT

The analyses presented in the previous chapters demonstrate that school choice has the potential to create more diverse schools even as it can also segregate and stratify them. The question of whether some school choice plans have caused schools to become more segregated will likely continue to be part of policy and research debates, but it takes a particularly strong ideology to argue that as a whole, these reforms have helped public schools to become more diverse. The policy question we should consider, then, is not whether we want school choice but, rather, what kinds of choices we will afford to students (Tyack, 1999). If we indeed desire both choice and student diversity, we would be wise to consider the range of choice options likely to produce schools that are racially and economically diverse and are open to students of different ability levels.

School choice, as a set of reforms, is not likely to decrease in popularity, despite the debates about the merits of choice options. As we move beyond policy rhetoric, we can best serve students by examining under what conditions choice helps to diversify student populations so that we can remedy school choice plans that have segregative effects within choice schools and traditional public schools alike. Of course efforts to maintain or increase student diversity cannot simply be a numbers game—effectively mixing bodies—in fact, early integrationists had a more comprehensive vision beyond desegregation and envisioned diverse schools that gave all children access to high-stakes knowledge through well-resourced schools (Kluger, 1975). They did not intend for students to be resegregated through tracking, special education, or racially homogenous classes once they entered the school doors, yet these were the very conditions under which too many children experienced desegregation.

Although school choice advocates rightly argue that we should emphasize quality of education rather than simple diversity, it is a sign of our politically polarized times that diversity is seen as anathema to school quality. Is there not room in the midst of policy debates to imagine public education systems that provide high-quality schooling with myriad options while also preserving and reaffirming the importance of diversity for social cohesion?

To envision such a possibility, we must face the current reality of racially and economically segregated schools. Many school districts do not have a legal obligation or the organizational capacities to ensure racial and ethnic balance in their schools, even though most remain highly segregated by race, socioeconomic class, and, increasingly, language. And poverty continues to shape schooling conditions in the both public and private spheres. In both arenas, schools serving high-poverty students of color often lack crucial resources, such as certified teachers, safe and clean facilities, advanced-placement courses, and adequate funding (Anyon, 1997; Kahlenberg, 2000; Kantor & Brenzel, 1993; Kozol, 1991; Scott & Holme, 2002). In this context, high-stakes accountability measures almost ensure that the schools serving children labeled as low achieving will not be attractive choices for other parents or high-quality teachers and school leaders. The most educationally vulnerable children could be further isolated with an expansion of school choice that does not also attend to diversity in student populations.

Even as we seek to increase choices and form more-diverse schools, one can argue that there remains space in the public sphere for school communities shaped around a particular pedagogical interest, educational concern, or cultural frame. Marginalized populations, those left most vulnerable by public and private institutions, have found respite in some of the choice options afforded them—especially in the case of charter schools. While diversity is a compelling goal, these schools should not necessarily be asked to join mainstream schooling structures. Still, these school communities should have choice plans that encourage equitable access and provide adequate resources. In addition, policymakers could craft choice plans that provide resource incentives for creating and maintaining diverse student bodies.

Even after the 50th anniversary of the *Brown* decision, parents and school communities find themselves negotiating school choice options against a complicated history of racial and social class exclusion in cities, suburbs, and rural areas where vestiges of racial and class segregation are still a reality. In 1960, W. E. B. Du Bois estimated that by the year 2000, school segregation in America on the basis of race would no longer exist (Du Bois, 1973). Alhough we are several years past his optimistic estimate, and indeterminately far away from this goal, perhaps a reevaluation of the educational policies we craft can help us to create more-imaginative choices that also encourage student diversity.

A central theme connecting the chapters in this volume has been that the social, legal and political contexts of school choice determine what effect choice plans can have on student diversity. Thus, this collection informs our understanding of the conditions under which school choice can increase or decrease student diversity, so that those interested in preserving social integration while also expanding meaningful choice options can proceed with an understanding of how to best approach that complicated task. To paraphrase Dubois (1960), such a task calls for "intelligence, cooperation, and careful planning."

# References

Ahearn, E. M. (1999). *Charter schools and special education: A report on state policies.* Washington, DC: Office of Special Education Programs. Available at: http://www.uscharterschools.org/pub/uscs_docs/fr/sped_policies.htm.

Ahearn, E. M., Lange, C. M., Rhim, L. M., & McLaughlin, M. J. (2001). Project SEARCH: Final Report. National Association of State Directors of Special Education. Available at http://www.nasdse.org/Project%20Search/project_search_documents.htm.

Allison, P. (1978). Measures of inequality. *American Sociological Review, 43*(6), 865–880.

American Association of University Women (AAUW). (1992). *How schools short-change girls.* Washington, DC: Harris Scholastic Research.

American Association of University Women (AAUW). (1998a). *Gendergaps: Where schools still fail our children.* Washington, DC: Harris Scholastic Research.

American Association of University Women (AAUW). (1998b). *Separated by sex: A critical look at single sex education for girls.* Washington, DC: Harris Scholastic Research.

American Association of University Women (AAUW). (2000). *Tech-savvy: Educating girls in the new computer age.* Washington, DC: Author.

American Association of University Women Educational Foundation. (1993). *Hostile hallways: The AAUW survey on sexual harassment in America's schools.* Washington, DC: Harris Scholastic Research.

Anyon, J. (1997). *Ghetto schooling: A political economy of urban educational reform.* New York: Teachers College Press.

Apple, M. W. (2002). Strange allies: Multicultural conservatism in America. *Educational Policy, 16*(2), 338–346.

Armor, D., Rossell, C., & Walberg, H. (2003). The outlook for school desegregation. In C. Rossell, D. Armor, & H. Walberg (Eds.), *Desegregation in the 21st century* (pp. 321–334). Westport, CT: Praeger.

Arons, S. (1989). Educational choice as a civil rights strategy. In N. E. Devins (Ed.), *Public values, private schools* (pp. 63–87). London: Falmer.

Arsen, D., Plank, D., & Sykes, G. (1999). *School choice policies in Michigan: The rules matter.* East Lansing: Michigan State University.

Artiles, A., & Trent, S. (1994). Overrepresentation of minority students in special education: A continuing debate. *The Journal of Special Education, 27*(4), 410–437.

Ascher, C., Jacobowitz, R., & McBride, Y. (1998, February). *Charter school access: A preliminary analysis of charter school legislation and charter school students* (Report to the Annie E. Casey Foundation). New York: New York University, Institute for Education and Social Policy.

Ascher, C., Jacobowitz, R., McBride, Y. & Wamba, N. (2000). *Going Charter: Lessons from Two First-Year Studies.* New York: New York University, The Institute for Education and Social Policy.

Ball, M. (2001, August 2). Desire for diversity in schools is at odds with recent rulings. *Washington Post*, p. 4.

Bankston, K., & Caldas, S. (2002). *A troubled dream: The promise and failure of school desegregation in Louisiana.* Nashville: Vanderbilt University Press.

Bankston, C., & Caldas, S. (2003). *The end of desegregation?* San Francisco: Lawrence Erlbaum.

Barnes, R. (1997). Black America and school choice: Charting a new course. *Yale Law Journal, 106*(8), 2375–2409.

Barrett, E. J., Taebel, D., Thurlow-Brenner, C., Kemmerer, F., Ausbrooks, C., Clark, C., Thomas, K., Briggs, K. L., Parker, A., Wieher, G., Matland, R., Tedin, K., Cookson, C., & Nielsen, L. (1997, December). *Texas open-enrollment charter schools: Year one evaluation.* Arlington: Texas State Board of Education.

Belenky, M. F., et al. (1986). *Women's ways of knowing: The development of self, voice, and mind.* New York: Basic Books.

Belk. v. Charlotte-Mecklenburg Board of Education, U.S.-122 S. Ct. 1538, 152 L.Ed.2d 465 (April 15, 2002).

*Birch Single Gender Academies Proposal.* (1997). Sacramento: California Department of Education.

Board of Education v. Booth, 984 P.2d 639 (Colo. 1999).

Board of Education v. Rowley, 458 U.S. 176 (1982). Center for Education Reform (2000).

Boger, J. (2002). A quick look at the remedial responsibilities under the federal constitution for school districts found to have practices *de jure* or intentional segregation of their public schools—and at judicial considerations of the relation between continuing school segregation and private housing choices in formerly segregated school districts. Unpublished manuscript. University of North Carolina, School of Law.

Boger, J. (2003). Education's "perfect storm"? Racial resegregation, high stakes testing, and school resource inequities: The case of North Carolina. *North Carolina Law Review, 81*(4), 1375–1462.

Boozer, M., Krueger, A., & Wolkon, S. (1992). Race and school quality since *Brown v. Board of Education. Brookings Papers on Economic Activity, Microeconomics*, Working paper number W4109, pp. 269–338.

Borjas, G. J. (1995). Ethnicity, neighborhoods, and human-capital externalities. *American Economic Review, 85*(3), 365–390.

Braddock, J. H. (1980). The perpetuation of segregation across levels of education: A behavioral assessment of the contact hypothesis. *Sociology of Education, 53*, 178–186.

Braddock, J. H., Crain, R. L., & McPartland, J. M. (1984). A long-term view of school desegregation: Some recent studies of graduates as adults. *Phi Delta Kappan, 66*(4), 259–264.

Braddock, J. H., & Eitle, T. (2003). The effects of school desegregation. In J. Banks & C. Banks (Ed.), *Handbook of research on multicultural education* (2nd ed.). San Francisco: Jossey-Bass.

Braddock, J. H., & McPartland, J. M. (1988). The social and academic consequences of school desegregation. *Equity and Choice, 4*(2), 5–10, 63–73.

Breed, A. (2002, January 2). 1-race schools gain new champions. Advocates look back, say desegregation proved to be a failure. *Charlotte-Observer,* p. 5B.

Brown, S. (1999, August). High school racial composition: Balancing excellence and equity. Paper presented at the meeting of the American Sociological Association, Chicago.

Brown v. Board of Education I, 347 U.S. 483 (1954).

Buddin, R. J., Cordes, J. J., & Kirby, S. N. (1998). School choice in California: Who chooses private schools? *Journal of Urban Economics, 44,* 110–134.

Bureau of the Census. (1992). *Current Population Survey, October 1998, 1999, 2000.* Washington, DC: Author.

Bureau of the Census. (2000). *Current population surveys 1998,1999, and 2000.*

California Department of Education. (1997). *Fact sheet: Single gender academies pilot program.* Sacramento, CA: Author.

California Education Code, Section 58520–58524. *Single gender academies pilot program.* Sacramento, CA: Author.

Capacchione et al. v. Charlotte-Mecklenburg Schools, U.S. 122 S. Ct. 1537, 152L.Ed.2d 465 (April 15, 2002).

Capacchione et al. v. Charlotte-Mecklenburg Board of Education, 57 F. Supp.2d 228 (W.D.N.C.1999).

Carl, J. (1996). Unusual allies: Elite and grass-roots origins of parent choice in Milwaukee. *Teachers College Record, 98*(2), 266–284.

Center for Applied Research and Educational Improvement. (1998). *Minnesota charter schools evaluation.* Minneapolis: University of Minnesota, College of Education and Human Development.

Center for Educational Reform. (2005). *Charter school laws: State by state ranking and profiles.* Washington, DC: Author.

Charlotte-Mecklenburg Schools (CMS). (1970–2002). *Monthly membership reports.* Charlotte, NC: Author.

Charlotte-Mecklenburg Schools (CMS). (1992, March 31). *Minutes of the school board meeting.* Charlotte, NC: Author.

Charlotte-Mecklenburg Schools (CMS). (1996–2002). *Class counts.* Charlotte, NC: Author.

Charlotte-Mecklenburg Schools (CMS). (2001a, April 3). *Board resolution 2001.* Charlotte, NC: Author. Available at www.cms.k12.nc.us/studentassignment/boardresolution2001.asp

Charlotte-Mecklenburg Schools (CMS). (2001b, July 31). *Board resolution 2002–2003.* Charlotte, NC: Author. Available at www.cms.k12.nc.us/studentassignment/boardresolution02–03.asp

Charlotte-Mecklenburg Schools (CMS). (2001c, July 30). *2002–2003 student assignment plan*. Charlotte, NC: Author.

Charlotte-Mecklenburg Schools. (2002a). *Demographics*. Charlotte, NC: Author.

Charlotte-Mecklenburg Schools. (2002b). *Teacher statistics as of May 22, 2002*. Charlotte, NC: Author.

Charlotte-Mecklenburg Schools. (2002, 2003). *Choice lottery results*. Charlotte, NC: Author.

Charlotte-Mecklenburg Schools (2003). *The history of public schools in Charlotte Mecklenburg*. Charlotte, NC: Author. Available at www.cms.k12.nc.us/discover/history.asp

Charter schools and special ed law: An imperfect union. (1996). *The Special Educator, 12*(7), 11.

Chermerinsky, E. (2003). The segregation and resegregation of American public education: The courts' role. *North Carolina Law Review, 81*, 1597–1622.

Chubb, J., & Moe, T. (1990). *Politics, markets, and America's schools*. Washington, DC: Brookings Institute.

Chubb, J., & Moe, T. (1996). Politics, markets, and equality in schools. In M. R. Darby (Ed.), *Reducing poverty in America* (pp. 121–153). Thousand Oaks, CA: Sage.

Clotfelter, C. (1976). School desegregation, "tipping," and private school enrollment. *Journal of Human Resources, 11*(1), 28–50.

Clotfelter, C. (1999). Public school segregation in metropolitan areas, *Land Economics, 75*, 487–504.

Clotfelter, C. (2001, Spring). Are Whites still "fleeing"? Racial patterns and enrollment shifts in urban public schools, 1987–1996. *Journal of Policy Analysis and Management, 20*. 199–221.

Cobb, C., & Glass, G. (1999). Ethnic segregation in Arizona charter schools. *Education Policy Analysis Archives, 7*(1). Available at http:www//epaa.asu.edu/epaa/v7n1/

Coeyman. M. (2001, January 9). One mold charters can't break. *The Christian Science Monitor*. Available online at: http://csmonitor.com/cgi-bin/durableRedirect.pl?/durable/2001/01/09/text/p11s1.html

Coleman, J., et al. (1966). *Equality of educational opportunity* (Department of Health, Education, and Welfare). Washington, DC: Government Printing Office.

Coleman, J. S., Hoffer, T., & Kilgore, S. (1982a, April/July). Achievement and segregation in secondary schools: A further look at public and private school differences. *Sociology of Education, 55*, 162–182.

Coleman, J., Hoffer, T., & Kilgore, S. (1982b). *High school achievement*. New York: Basic Books.

Common Core of Data. (1997–1998). *Public elementary/secondary school universe survey: School year 1997–98*. Washington, DC: Department of Education, Office of Educational Research and Improvement.

Colorado Department of Education. (2002, April). *The state of charter schools in Colorado, 2000–01*. Denver, CO: Author. Available at http://www.cde.state.co.us/cdechart/charsurv.htm.

Conlon, J. R., & Kimenyi, M. S. (1991, Fall). Attitudes toward race and poverty in the demand for private education: The Case of Mississippi. *The Review of Black Political Economy, 20,* 4–22.

Cookson, P. W., Jr. (1994). *School choice: The struggle for the soul of American education.* New Haven, CT: Yale University Press.

Crain, R. (1984). *Private schools and Black-White segregation: Evidence from two big cities.* Stanford: Stanford University, Institute for Research on Educational Finance and Government. (ERIC Document no. 259430)

Crain, R. L., & Mahard, R. E. (1978). School racial composition and Black college attendance and achievement test performance. *Sociology of Education, 51*(2), 81–100.

Crain, R. L., & Mahard, R. E. (1981). Some policy implications of the desegregation–minority achievement literature. In W. D. Hawley (Ed.), *Effective school desegregation: Equity, quality, and feasibility* (pp. 55–84). Beverly Hills, CA: Sage.

Crain, R. L., & Mahard, R. E. (1983). The effect of research methodology on desegregation-achievement studies: A meta-analysis. *American Journal of Sociology, 88*(5), 839–854.

Crain, R. L., Miller, R. L., Hawes, J. A., & Peichert, J. R. (1992). Finding niches: Desegregated students 16 years later. *Final Report on the Educational Outcomes of Project Concern, Hartford, Connecticut.* New York: Institute for Urban and Minority Education, Teachers College, Columbia University.

Crain, R. L., & Strauss, J. (1985). *School segregation and Black occupational attainments: Results from a long-term experiment* (Report No. 359). Baltimore: Center for the Social Organization of Schools.

Cready, C. M., & Fossett, M. A. (1998). The impact of desegregation on White public school enrollment in the U.S. nonmetro South, 1960–1990. *Social Science Quarterly, 79,* 664–676.

Current Population Surveys. (1998–2000). *School enrollment—Social and economic characteristics of students.* Washington, DC: United States Bureau of the Census.

Cutler, D. M., & Glaeser, E. L. (1997, August). Are ghettos good or bad? *Quarterly Journal of Economics, 112,* 827–872.

Darling-Hammond, L. (2000). Teacher quality and student achievement: A review of state policy evidence. *Education Policy Analysis Archives, 8*(1), 1–50. Available at http://epaa.edu/epaa/v8 n 1.

Datnow, A. (1998). *The gender politics of educational change.* London: Falmer.

Datnow, A., & Hubbard, L. (Eds.). (2002). *Gender in policy and practice: Perspectives on single-sex and coeducational schooling.* New York: RoutledgeFalmer.

Datnow, A., Hubbard, L., & Conchas, G. (2001). How context mediates policy: The implementation of single gender public schooling in California. *Teachers College Record, 103*(2), 184–206.

Datnow, A., Hubbard, L., & Woody, E. (2001). Is single gender schooling viable in the public sector? Lessons from California's pilot program. Final report. Toronto, Ontario: Ontario Institute for Studies in Education. Available at http://www.oise.utoronto.ca/depts/tps/adatnow/research.html#single

Diana v. State Board of Education, Civ. No. 70–37, consent decree (N.D.Cal. 1970).

Douglas, D. M. (1995). *Reading, writing, and race: The desegregation of the Charlotte schools*. Chapel Hill: University of North Carolina Press.

Du Bois, W. E. B. (1935). Does the Negro need separate schools? *The Journal of Negro Education, 4*(3), 328–335.

Du Bois, W. E. B. (1973). Whither now and why. In H. Aptheker (Ed.), *The education of Black people: Ten critiques, 1906–1960*. Amherst: University of Massachusetts Press.

Duncan, G., & Brooks-Gunn, J. (1997). *Consequences of growing up poor*. New York: Russell Sage Foundation.

Dwyer, J. G. (2002). *Vouchers Within reason*. Ithaca, NY: Cornell University Press.

Easton, J. Q., & Bennett, A. (1989, April). *Some effects of voluntary transfer on predominantly minority sending schools*. Paper presented to the annual meetings of the American Educational Research Association, San Francisco.

Eaton, S. (1999). *Memories of METCO: What do they tell us?* Unpublished manuscript.

Edsall, T. B., with Edsall, M. D. (1991). *Chain reaction: The impact of race, rights, and taxes on American politics*. New York: W. W. Norton.

Epple, D., & Romano, R. E. (1996). Ends against the middle: Determining public service provision when there are private alternatives. *Journal of Public Economics, 62*, 297–325.

Evans, W. N., Oates, W. E., & Schwab, R. M. Measuring peer group effects: A study of teenage behavior. *Journal of Political Economy, 100*(5), 966–991.

Farkas, S., Johnson, J., Immerwahr, S., & McHugh, J. (1998). *Time to move on: African-American and White parents set an agenda for public schools*. New York, NY: Public Agenda.

Farley, R., & Frey, W. H. (1994, February). Changes in the segregation of Whites from Blacks during the 1980s: Small steps toward a more integrated society. *American Sociological Review, 59*, 23–45.

Ferguson, R. F. (1998a). Can schools narrow the Black–White test score gap? In C. Jencks & M. Phillips (Eds.), *The Black–White test score gap* (pp. 318–374). Washington, DC: Brookings Institute.

Finn, C. (1991). *We must take charge: Our schools and our future*. New York: Free Press.

Finn, C. E., Manno, B. V., & Vanourek, G. (2000). *Charter schools in action: Renewing public education*. Princeton, NJ: Princeton University Press.

Fiore, T. A., & Cashman, E. R. (1998). *Review of charter school legislation provisions related to students with disabilities*. Washington, DC: Office of Educational Research and Improvement.

Fiske, E., & Ladd, H. (2000). *When schools compete*. Washington, DC: Brookings Institute.

Fowler, F. C. (2003). School choice: Silver bullet, social threat, or sound policy? *Educational Researcher, 32*(2), 33–39.

Frankenberg, E., & Lee, C. (2002). *Race in American public schools: Rapidly resegre-*

*gating school districts*. Cambridge, MA: The Civil Rights Project at Harvard University.

Frankenberg, E., & Lee, C. (2003). *Charter schools and race: A lost opportunity for integrated education*. Cambridge, MA: The Civil Rights Project at Harvard University.

Fuller, B. (Ed.). (2000). *Inside charter schools: The paradox of radical decentralization*. Cambridge, MA: Harvard University Press.

Fuller, B., Elmore, R., & Orfield, G. (Eds.). (1996). *Who chooses? who loses? Culture, institutions, and the unequal effects of school choice*. New York: Teachers College Press.

Fuller, H. (2000, March). *The continuing struggle of African Americans for the power to make real educational choices*. Paper presented at the Second Annual Symposium on Educational Options for African Americans.

Fuller, H., & Mitchell, G. (1999). *The impact of school choice on racial and ethnic enrollment in Milwaukee private schools* (Marquette University Institute for the Transformation of Learning, Current Education Issues, No. 99–5). Milwaukee, WI: Marquette University.

Fusarelli, L. D. (2000, April). *Texas: Charter schools and the struggle for equity*. Paper presented at the annual meeting of the American Education Research Association, New Orleans.

Garn, G. A. (2000, October 12). Arizona charter schools: A case study of values and school policy. *Current Issues in Education, 3*(7). Available at http://cie.ed.asu.edu/volume3/number7/.

Gewirtz, S., Ball, S. J., & Bowe, R. (1995). *Markets, choice, and equity in education*. Bristol, PA: Open University Press.

Gilbert, R., & Gilbert, P. (1998). *Masculinity goes to school*. London: Routledge.

Gilligan, C. (1982). *In a different voice*. Cambridge, MA: Harvard University Press.

Ginorio, A. M., & Huston, M. (2001). *Sí, we puede! Yes, we can: Latinas in school*. Washington, DC: American Association of University Women.

Gipps. C. (1996). Introduction. In P. F. Murphy & C. V. Gibbs (Eds.), *Equity in the classroom: Towards effective pedagogy for girls and boys* (pp. 1–6). London: Falmer.

Glatter, R., Woods, P. A., & Bagley, C. (1997). Diversity, differentiation, and hierarchy: School choice and parental preferences. In R. Glatter, P. A. Woods, & C. Bagley (Eds.), *Choice and diversity in schooling* (pp. 7–28). London: Routledge.

Glazerman, S. (1998, April). *School quality and social stratification: The determinants and consequences of parental school choice*. Paper presented at the annual meeting of the American Educational Research Association, San Diego.

Godwin, R. K., & Kemerer, F. (2002). *School choice tradeoffs: Liberty, equity, and diversity*. Austin: University of Texas Press.

Goldhaber, D. D. (1996). Public and private high schools: Is school choice an answer to the productivity problem? *Economics of Education Review, 15*(2), 93–109.

Good, T. L., & Braden, J. S. (2000). *Charting a new course: Fact and fiction about charter schools*. Alexandria, VA: National School Boards Association.

Green, J. P., & Mellow, N. (1998). Integration where it counts: A study of racial integration in public and private school lunchrooms. *School Choices*. Available at www.schoolchoices.org/roo/jay1.htm.

Greene, J. (1998). Civic values in public and private schools. In P. Peterson & B. Hassel (Eds.), *Learning from school choice*. Washington, DC: Brookings.

Greene, J. (1999, September). The racial, economic, and religious context of parental choice in Cleveland. Paper presented at the meeting of the Association for Public Policy Analysis and Management, Washington, DC. Available at http://hdc.www.harvard.edu/pepg/index.htm.

Greene, J., & Mellow, N. (1998). *Integration where it counts: A study of racial integration in public and private school lunchrooms* (Public Policy Clinic Working Paper). Available at http://www.la.utexas.edu/research/ppc/lunch.html.

Greenwald, R., Hedges, L. V., & Laine, R. D. (1994). The effect of school resources on students' achievement. *Review of Educational Research, 66,* 361–396.

Grissmer, D. W., Flanagan, A., & Williamson, S. (1998). Why did the Black–White score gap narrow in the 1970s and 1980s? In C. Jencks & M. Phillips (Eds.), *The Black–White Test Score Gap* (pp. 182–228). Washington, DC: Brookings.

Grutter v. Bollinger et al. 539 U.S. (2003).

Gurian, M. (1998). *A fine young man: What parents, mentors and educators can do to shape adolescent boys into exceptional men*. New York: Putnam.

Hallinan, M. T. (1998). Diversity effects on student outcomes: Social science evidence. *Ohio State Law Journal, 59,* 733–754.

Hanushek, E. (1997). Assessing the effects of school resources on student performance: An update. *Educational Evaluation and Policy Analysis, 19,* 141–164.

Hanushek, E., & Quigley, J. (1978b). Housing market disequilibrium and residential mobility. In W.A.V. Clark & E. G. Moore (Eds.), *Population mobility and residential change* (pp. 51–98). Studies in Geography 25. Evanston, IL: Northwestern University.

Hanushek, E., & Quigley, J. (1978a). An explicit model of intra-metropolitan mobility, *Land Economics, 54,* 411–429.

Hawley, R. (1993). The case for boys schools. In D. K. Hollinger & R. Adamson (Eds.), *Single sex schooling: Proponents speak* (pp. 11–14). Washington, DC: U.S. Department of Education.

Hawley, W. (2002). *Diversity and educational quality* (Unpublished manuscript). School of Education, University of Maryland, College Park.

Hedges, L. V., Laine, R. D., & Greenwald, R. (1994). Does money matter? A meta analysis of studies of the effects of differential inputs on student outcomes. *Educational Researcher, 23,* 5–14.

Heise, M., & Nechyba, T. (1999). School finance reform: A case for vouchers. *Civic Report, 9.* New York: Center for Civic Innovation, The Manhattan Institute for Public Policy Research.

Helms, A. D. (2002, March 20). Blacks less likely to get choice of schools. *Charlotte Observer*, p. 1A.

Helms, A. D. (2003a, March 24). In-demand schools shut choice door. *Charlotte Observer*, p. 1A.

Helms, A. D. (2003b, January 5). Parents' choice may clinch schools' fate. *Charlotte Observer*, p. 4A.

Hendrie, C. (1999a, March 24). In black and white. *Education Week on the Web*. Available at www.edweek.org/ew/articles/1999/03/24/28deseg.h18.html ?querystring=in%20black%20white.

Hendrie, C. (1999b, July 14). Race-based assignment challenged. *Education Week on the Web*. Available at www.edweek.org/ew/articles/1999/07/14/42deseg. h18.html?querystring=race-based%20assignment%20challenged.

Henig, J. (1994). *Rethinking school choice. Limits of the market metaphor*. Princeton, NJ: Princeton University Press.

Henig, J. (1996). The local dynamics of choice. In B. Fuller & R. Elmore (Eds.), *Who chooses? Who loses?* New York: Teachers College Press.

Henig, J. R., & Sugarman, S. D. (1999). The nature and extent of school choice. In S. D. Sugarman & F. R. Kemerer (Eds.), *School choice and social controversy* (pp. 13–35). Washington, DC: Brookings.

Heubert, J. P. (1997). Schools without rules? Charter schools, federal disability law, and the paradoxes of deregulation. *Harvard Civil Rights–Civil Liberties Law Review, 32*, 301–353.

Hobson v. Hansen, 269 F.Supp. 401 (D.D.C. 1967), aff'd sub nom. Smuck v. Hobson, 408 F.2d 175 (D.C. Cir. 1969).

Hochschild, J., & Scrovronik, N. (2003). *The American dream and the public schools*. New York: Oxford University Press.

Holme, J. J. (2002). Buying homes, buying schools: School choice and the social construction of school quality. *Harvard Educational Review, 72*(2), 177–201.

Holt, M. (2000). *Not yet "free at last": The unfinished business of the civil rights movement*. Oakland, CA: Institute for Contemporary Studies.

Hopkins, R. (1997). *Educating Black males: Critical lessons in schooling, community, and power*. Albany: State University of New York Press.

Horn, J., & Miron, G. (1999). *Evaluation of the Michigan public school academy initiative*. East Lansing: The Evaluation Center, Western Michigan University.

Howe, K. R., & Eisenhart, M. (2000). *A study of the Boulder Valley School District's open enrollment policy* (Technical Report). Boulder, CO: Authors.

Howe, K. R. & Welner, K. G. (2002). The school choice movement: Déjà vu for children with disabilities? *Remedial and Special Education, 23*(4), 212–221.

Hubbard, L., & Datnow, A. (2002). Are single gender schools sustainable in the public sector? In A. Datnow & L. Hubbard (Eds.), *Gender in policy and practice: Perspectives on single-sex and coeducational schooling*. New York: Routledge Falmer.

Hutchison, K. B. (1999, October 6). Senate floor speech on single-sex classrooms amendment. Proceedings and debates of the 106th congress, first session. Available at http://www.senate.gov/hutchison/speech11.htm

Ingersoll, R. (1999). The problem of underqualified teachers in American secondary schools. *Educational Researcher, 28*, 26–37.

James, D. R., & Taeuber, K. E. (1985). Measures of segregation. In N. B. Tuma (Ed.), *Sociological methodology* (Vol. 14, pp. 1–32). San Francisco: Jossey-Bass.

Jennings, W., Premack, E., Adelmann, A., & Solomon, D. (1998). *A comparison of charter school legislation*. Washington, DC: U.S. Department of Education, RPP International.

Johnston, S. (2003, March 1). A door slams shut: Board's guarantee of choice-out of high-poverty schools has disappeared. *Educate!*, 3–5. Available at www.educateclt.org/archives.asp

Kahlenberg, R. D. (Ed.). (2000). *A notion at risk*. New York: The Century Foundation Press.

Kahlenberg, R. D. (2001). *All together now: Creating middle-class schools through public school choice*. Washington, DC: Brookings Institute.

Kantor, H., & Brenzel, B. (1993). Urban education and the "truly disadvantaged": The historical roots of the contemporary crisis, 1945–1990. In M. Katz (Ed.), *The "underclass' debate: Views from history* (pp. 366–402). Princeton, NJ: Princeton University Press.

Kleinfeld, J. (1999). Student performance: Males versus females. *The Public Interest, 134*, 3–20.

Kluger, R. (1975). *Simple justice*. New York: Vintage Books.

Kozol, J. (1991). *Savage inequalities*. New York: Crown.

Kruse, A. M. (1996). Single sex settings: Pedagogies for girls and boys in Danish schools. In P. Murphy & G. Gipps (Eds.), *Equity in the classroom: Towards effective pedagogy for girls and boys* (pp. 173–191). London: Falmer.

Ladd, H. F., & Fiske E. B. (1999). *The uneven playing field of school choice: Evidence from New Zealand* Unpublished manuscript.

Lange, C. M. (1997). *Charter schools and special education: A handbook*. Alexandria, VA: National Association of State Directors of Special Education.

Lange, C. M., & Lehr, C. A. (2000). Charter schools and students with disabilities: Parent perceptions of reasons for transfer and satisfaction with services. *Remedial and Special Education, 21*, 141.

Lankford, H., Lee, E., & Wyckoff, J. (1995). An analysis of elementary and secondary school choice. *Journal of Urban Economics, 38*, 236–251.

Lankford, H., & Wyckoff, J. (1992). Primary and secondary school choice among public and religious alternatives. *Economics of Education Review, 11*(4), 317–337.

Lankford, H., & Wyckoff, J. (1995). Property taxation, taxpayer burden, and local educational finance in New York. *Journal of Education Finance, 21*, 57–86

Lankford, H., & Wyckoff, J. (1997). School choice: Who is likely to be left behind (Working Paper). Albany: State University of New York Press.

Lankford, H., & Wyckoff, J. (1999). *The effect of school choice and residential location on the racial segregation of elementary students* (Working Paper.). Albany: State University of New York Press.

Lankford, H., & Wykoff, J. H. (2000, May 22). *Why are schools racially segregated? Implications for school choice policies*. Paper prepared for the School Choice and Racial Diversity Conference, Teachers College, Columbia University, New York, sponsored by the National Center for the Study of Privatization and the Civil Rights Project.

Larry P. v. Riles, 793 F.2d 969 (9th Cir. 1984).

Leake, D., & Leake, B. (1992). Islands of hope: Milwaukee's African American immersion schools. *Journal of Negro Education, 61*(1), 24–29.

Lee, V., & Bryk, A. S. (1986). Effects of single sex schools on student achievement and attitudes. *Journal of Educational Psychology, 78*, 381–395.

Lee, V. E., & Burkam, D. T. (2002). *Inequality at the starting gate: Social background and achievement at kindergarten entry.* Washington, DC: Educational Policy Institute.

Lee, V., Croninger, R., & Smith, J. (1996). Equity and choice in Detroit. In B. Fuller & R. F. Elmore (Eds.), *Who chooses, Who loses: Culture, institutions, and the unequal effects of school choice.* New York: Teachers College Press.

Levin, B. (1999). Race and school choice. In S. D. Sugarman & F. R. Kemerer (Eds.), *School choice and social controversy* (pp. 266–299). Washington, DC: Brookings Institution.

Levin, H. (1998). Educational vouchers: Effectiveness, choice, and costs. *Journal of Policy Analysis and Management, 17*(3), 373–392.

Levin, H. (2000). *A comprehensive framework for evaluating educational vouchers.* (Occasional Papers Series, National Center for the Study of Privatization in Education, Teachers College, No. 5), 1–39. New York: Teachers College.

Lissitz, R. W. (1993, December). *Assessment of student performance and attitude, year III–1993: St. Louis metropolitan area court-ordered desegregation effort* (Report Submitted to the Voluntary Interdistrict Coordinating Council). St. Louis, MO: Voluntary Interdistrict Coordinating Council.

Lissitz, R. W. (1994, December). *Assessment of student performance and attitude, year IV—1994: St. Louis metropolitan area court-ordered desegregation effort* (Report Submitted to the Voluntary Interdistrict Coordinating Council). St. Louis, MO: Voluntary Interdistrict Coordinating Council.

Losen, D., & Welner, K. G. (2001). Disabling discrimination in our public schools: Comprehensive legal challenges to inappropriate and inadequate special education services for minority children. *Harvard Civil Rights–Civil Liberties Law Review, 36*(2), 407–460.

Lucas, S. R. (1999). *Tracking inequality.* New York: Teachers College Press.

Mael, F. (1998). Single sex and coeducational schooling: Relationships to socioemotional and academic development. *Review of Educational Research, 68*, 101–129.

Manski, C. F. (1993). Identification of endogenous social effects: The reflection problem. *Review of Economic Studies, 60*, 531–542.

Marshall, C., Mitchell, D., & Wirt, F. (1989). *Culture and education policy in the American states.* New York: Falmer.

Massey, D. S., & Denton, N. A. (1988). The dimensions of racial segregation. *Social Forces, 67*(2), 281–315.

Massey, D. S., & Denton, N. A. (1993). *American apartheid: Segregation and the making of the underclass.* Cambridge, MA: Harvard University Press.

Massey, D. S., & Hazal, Z. (1995, September). The changing geographic structure of Black–White segregation in the United States, *Social Science Quarterly, 76*, 527–542.

McEwan, P. J., & Carnoy, M. (1998). *Choice between private and public schools in a voucher system: Evidence from Chile.* Unpublished manuscript.

McKinney, J. R. (1996). Charter schools: A new barrier for children with disabilities. *Educational Leadership, 54*(22), 22–25.

McKinney, J. R. (1998, August). Charter schools' legal responsibilities toward children with disabilities. *West's Education Law Reporter, 126,* 565–576.

McKinney, J. R., & Mead, J. F. (1996). Law and policy in conflict: Including students with disabilities in parental-choice programs. *Educational Administration Quarterly, 32*(1), 107–141.

McLaughlin, M. J., Henderson, K., & Ullah, H. (1996). *Charters schools and students with disabilities.* Alexandria, VA: Center for Policy Research.

Meier, K., Stewart, J., & England, R. (1989). *Race, class, and education: The politics of second generation discrimination.* Madison: University of Wisconsin Press.

Metcalf, K. K. (2001). *Evaluation of the Cleveland scholarship program.* Bloomington: Indiana Center for Evaluation.

Mickelson, R. A. (2001a, April). How middle school segregation contributes to the race gap in academic achievement. Paper presented at the annual meeting of the American Educational Research Association, Seattle.

Mickelson, R. A. (2001b). Subverting *Swann:* First- and second-generation segregation in the Charlotte Mecklenburg Schools. *American Educational Research Journal, 38,* 215–252.

Mickelson, R. A. (2003, August). *Segregation and the SAT.* Paper presented at the annual meeting of the American Sociological Association, Atlanta.

Mickelson, R. (2003). The academic consequences of desegregation and segregation: Evidence from the Charlotte-Mecklenburg schools. *North Carolina Law Journal, 81,* 1515–1562.

Mickelson, R. A., & Ray, C. A. (1994). Fear of falling from grace: The middle class, downward mobility, and school desegregation. *Research in Sociology of Education and Socialization, 10,* 207–238.

Mintrom, M., & Plank, D. N. (2000). *The emerging market for schooling: Evidence from Michigan.* Unpublished manuscript, Michigan State University.

Mirga, T. (1982, December 15). Civil-rights panel attacks Reagan's policy on busing. *Education Week on the Web.* Available at www.edweek.org/ew/articles/1982/12/15/03010013.h02.html?querystring=december%2015,%201982

Miron, G. (2000, April). *What's public about Michigan's charter schools: Lessons from school reform from statewide evaluations of charter schools.* Paper prepared for the annual meeting of the American Educational Research Association, New Orleans.

Miron, G., & Nelson, C. (2002). *What's public about charter schools? Lessons learned about choice and accountability.* Thousand Oaks, CA: Corwin.

Moore, M., Piper, V., & Schaefer, E. (1993). Single sex schooling and educational effectiveness: A research overview. In D. K. Hollinger (Ed.), *Single sex schooling: Perspectives from practice and research* (pp. 7–68). Washington, DC: U.S. Department of Education.

Morrill, J. (1999, April 18). Trial brings school case full circle. *Charlotte Observer,* p. 16A.

Mulholland, L. (1999). *Arizona charter school progress evaluation.* Phoenix, AZ: Morrison Institution for Public Policy.

Murphy, P., & Gipps, G. (Eds.). (1996). *Equity in the classroom: Towards effective pedagogy for girls and boys.* London: Falmer.

National Center for Education Statistics. (1992). *National Education Longitudinal Study.* Washington, DC: Department of Education, Office for Educational Research and Improvement.

National Center for Educational Statistics (NCES). (2001). *Digest of educational statistics, 2001.* Washington, DC: Department of Education, Office of Educational Research and Improvement.

National Center for Education Statistics. (2000a). *1997–1998 NCES Common Core of Data (CCD) public elementary and secondary school universe.* Washington, DC: Department of Education, Office of Educational Research and Improvement.

National Center for Education Statistics. (2000b). *1997–1998 NCES Private School Survey (PSS).* Washington, DC: Department of Education, Office of Educational Research and Improvement.

National Conference of State Legislatures. (1998). *Charter school legislative summary: 1998.* Available at http://www.ncsl.org/programs/educ/c1schls.htm #update.

Natriello, G. (1999, September 28). Address to the Charlotte-Mecklenburg School Board.

Natriello, G., McDill, E., & Pallas, A. (1990). *Schooling disadvantaged children. Racing against catastrophe.* New York: Teachers College Press.

Oakes, J., Muir, K., & Joseph, R. (2000, May). Course taking and achievement in math and science: Inequalities that endure. Paper presented at the conference of the National Institute for Science Education, Detroit.

Office of Civil Rights, United States Department of Education (1997). *Questions and answers on the application of federal civil rights laws to public charter schools.* Available at http://www.uscharterschools.org/pub/uscs_docs/fr/civil_rights_sub.htm.

Orfield, G. (1969). *The reconstruction of Southern education: The schools and the 1964 Civil Rights Act.* New York: John Wiley.

Orfield, G. (1978). *Must we bus? Segregated schools and national policy.* Washington, DC: Brookings Institution.

Orfield, G. (1983). *Public school desegregation in the United States, 1968–1980.* Washington, DC: Joint Center for Political Studies.

Orfield, G. (1994, December 8–9). Metropolitan school desegregation: Schools and urban change. In *Round Tables on Regionalism*, Social Science Research Council, U.S. Department of Housing and Urban Development (pp. 1–32).

Orfield, G. (2001). *Schools more separate: Consequences of a decade of resegregation.* Cambridge, MA: The Civil Rights Project at Harvard University.

Orfield, G., with Arenson, J., Jackson, T., Bohrer, C., Gavin, D., & Kalejs, E. (1997, September). City-suburban desegregation: Parent and student perspectives in metropolitan Boston. A report by the Harvard Civil Rights Project. *Equity and Excellence in Education, 31*(3), 6–12.

Orfield, G., & Ashkinaze, C. (1991). *The closing door: Conservative policy and Black opportunity.* Chicago: University of Chicago Press.

Orfield, G., Bachmeier, M., James, D., & Eitle, T. (1997). *Deepening segregation in American public schools.* Cambridge, MA: Harvard Project on School Desegregation.

Orfield, G., & Eaton, S. (1996). *Dismantling desegregation.* New York: The New Press.

Orfield, G., Glass, D., Reardon, S., & Schley, S. (1993). *The growth of segregation in American schools: Changing patterns of separation and poverty since 1968.* Cambridge, MA: Harvard Project on Desegregation.

Orfield, G., & Yun, J. T. (1999). *Resegregation in American schools.* Cambridge, MA: The Civil Rights Project.

Pachón, H., Tornatsky, L., & Torres, C. (2003). *Closing achievement gaps: Improving educational outcomes for Hispanic children.* Claremont, CA: The Center for Latino Educational Excellence, The Tomás Rivera Policy Institute.

Page, E., & Keith, T. (1981, August 10). Effects of U.S. private schools: A technical analysis of two recent claims. *Educational Researcher, 10*(7), 7–17.

Payne, K. J., & Biddle, B. K. (1999). Poor school funding, child poverty, and mathematics achievement. *Educational Researcher, 28,* 4–13.

Pearce, D. M. (1981). Deciphering the dynamics of school segregation: The role of schools in housing choice process. *The Urban Review, 13*(2), 85–99.

Pearce, N., Crain, R., Farley, R., & Taeuber, K. (1984, April). *Lessons not lost: The impact of school desegregation on the racial ecology of cities.* Paper presented at the annual meeting of the American Education Research Association, New Orleans.

Peterson, P., & Hassel, B. C. (1998). *Learning from school choice.* Washington, DC: Brookings Institution.

Pierce, R. (1999, August 29). Citizens panel required by desegregation pact has yet to be formed. *St. Louis Post-Dispatch,* p. C6.

Piliawsky, M. (1998). Remedies to de facto school segregation: The case of Hartford. *Black Scholar, 28*(2), 29–35.

Pipher, M. (1994). *Reviving Ophelia: Saving the selves of adolescent girls.* New York: Putnam.

Pleasants, H. M. (2000). *Defining and seeking a "good education": A qualitative study of Black parents who select charter schools for their children.* Unpublished doctoral dissertation, Michigan State University, East Lansing.

Pollack, W. (1998). *Real boys: Rescuing our sons from the myths of boyhood.* New York: Random House.

Pollard, D. S. (1998). The contexts of single sex classes. In S. Morse (Ed.), *Separated by sex: A critical look at single sex education for girls.* Washington, DC: American Association of University Women.

*Private School Survey.* (1997–1998). Washington, DC: Department of Education, Office of Educational Research and Improvement.

Public Policy Research Centers. (1993). *Perceptions of the transfer program: Focus group transcription: Parents of 11th grade transfer students* (Submitted to the

Voluntary Interdistrict Coordinating Council). St. Louis: University of Missouri–St. Louis.

Public Sector Consultants & MAXIMUS. (1997). *Michigan's charter school initiative: From theory to practice.* Available at http://www.mde.state.mi.us

Public Sector Consultants & MAXIMUS, Inc. (1999). *Michigan's charter school initiative: From theory to practice.* East Lansing: Michigan Department of Education.

Quigley, J. M. (1985). Consumer choice of dwelling, neighborhood, and public services. *Regional Science and Urban Economics, 15*, 41–63.

Quigley, J. M., & Weinberg, D. H. (1977). Intra-urban residential mobility: A review and synthesis. *International Regional Science Review, 2*, 41–66.

Rasell, E., & Rothstein, R. (Eds.). (1993). *School choice: Examining the evidence.* Washington, DC: Economic Policy Institute.

Ray, C. A., & Mickelson, R. A. (1990). Corporate leaders, resistant youth, and school reform in Sunbelt City: The political economy of education. *Social Problems, 37*(2), 178–190.

Reardon, S. (1998, March). *Measures of racial diversity and segregation in multi-group and hierarchically-structured populations.* Paper presented at the annual meeting of the Eastern Sociological Society, Philadelphia.

Reardon, S. F., & Firebaugh, G. (2002). Measures of multi-group segregation. *Sociological Methodology, 32*(1), 33–67.

Reardon, S. F., & Yun, J. T. (2000). The changing context of school segregation: Multiracial measurement of school segregation from 1987–1997. *Demography, 37*(3), 351–364.

Reardon, S., & Yun, J. (2002). *Private school enrollments and racial segregation.* Cambridge, MA: Harvard Civil Rights Project.

Reardon, S. F., Yun, J. T., & Eitle, T. M. (2000). The changing structure of school segregation: Measurement and evidence of multi-racial metropolitan area school segregation, 1989–1995. *Demography, 37*(3), 351–364.

Reschovshy, A. (1979). Residential choice and the local public sector: An alternative test of the "tiebout hypothesis," *Journal of Urban Economics, 6*, 501–520.

Reynolds, W. B. (1984). Remarks of assistant attorney general, civil rights division before the Metropolitan Center for Educational Research, Development and Training, New York University, *Brown* Plus Thirty Conference, New York.

Reynolds, W. B. (1986). Education alternatives to transportation failures: The desegregation response to a resegregation dilemma. *Metropolitan Education, 1*, 3–14.

Rhim, L. M., & McLaughlin, M. J. (2000). Charter schools and special education: Balancing disparate visions. Alexandria, VA: National Association of State Directors of Special Education. (Eric Document # ED 444 297).

Richards, C. (2000, November 15). Public funds for experimental single-sex ed? *Women's News.* Available at http://www.womensenews.org/article.cfm?aid =160&context=arcive.

Riordan, C. (1990). *Girls and boys in school: Together or separate?* New York: Teachers College Press.

Riordan, C. (1998, August). *Student outcomes in public secondary schools: Gender gap comparisons from 1972 to 1992.* Paper presented at the annual meeting of the American Sociological Association, San Francisco.

Ritter, G., Rush, A., & Rush, J. (2002, Spring). How might school choice affect racial integration in schools? *The Georgetown Public Policy Review, 72*(2), 125–136.

Rivkin, S. (1994, October). Residential segregation and school integration, *Sociology of Education, 67,* 279–292.

Rivkin, S. (1995). *School desegregation, academic attainment and employment* [Mimeo]. Department of Economics, Amherst College.

Rivkin, S. (1997). *The estimation of peer group effects* [Mimeo]. Department of Economics, Amherst College.

Rossell, C. (1987). The Buffalo controlled choice plan. *Urban Education, 22*(3), 328–354.

Rossell, C. (1990). *The carrot or the stick for school desgregation policy.* Philadelphia: Temple University Press.

Rossell, C. (1995, September). Controlled-choice desegregation plans: Not enough choice, too much control? *Urban Affairs Review, 31*(1), 43–76.

Rossell, C., & Glenn, C. L. (1988). The Cambridge controlled choice plan. *The Urban Review, 20*(2), 75–94.

Rothstein, R., Carnoy, M., & Benveniste, L. (1999). *Can public schools learn from private schools?: Case studies in the public and private nonprofit sectors.* Washington, DC: Economic Policy Institute.

RPP International. (1998). *A national study of charter schools: A second year report.* Washington, DC: U.S. Department of Education, Office of Educational Research and Improvement.

RPP International. (1999, May). *The state of charter schools. Third-year report.* Washington, DC: U.S. Department of Education, Office of Educational Research and Improvement.

RPP International. (2000). *The state of charter schools 2000: National study of charter schools.* Fourth-Year Report. Washington, DC: U.S. Department of Education, Office of Educational Research and Improvement.

RPP International & the University of Minnesota. (1997). *A study of charter schools: Third-year report.* Washington, DC: US Department of Education, Office of Educational Research and Improvement.

Ryan, J. E., & Heise, M. (2002). The political economy of school choice. *Yale Law Journal, 111*(2043), 87.

Sadker, M., & Sadker, D. (1994). *Failing at fairness.* New York: Touchstone.

Saporito, S. J., & Lareau, A. (1999). School selection as a process: The multiple dimensions of race in framing educational choice. *Social Problems, 46,* 418–439.

Savage, D. (2000, March 21). Justices cast doubt on school race balancing. *The Los Angeles Times,* pp. A1, A9.

Schelling, T. C. (1971). Dynamic models of segregation. *Journal of Mathematical Sociology, 1,* 143–186.

Schnaiberg, L. (2000, May 10). Charter schools: Choice, diversity may be at odds. *Education Week, 19*(1), 18–20.

Schneider, M., Teske, P., Marschall, M., & Roch, D. (1997, Fall). School choice builds community. *Public Interest, 129*, pp. 86–90.

Scott, J., & Holme, J. J. (2002). Public schools, private resources: The role of social networks in California charter school reform. In A. S. Wells (Ed.), *When public policy comes up short: Charter schools, accountability, and equity* (pp. 102–128). New York: Teachers College Press.

Shujaa, M. (1993). *Too much schooling, too little education: The paradox of Black life in White societies.* Trenton, NJ: Africa World Press.

Simmons, R. (2004, September 24). 'Crisis' is Suburbanites' Creation. *Educate!* Available at www.educateclt.org.

Smith, K. B., & Meier, K. J. (1995). *The case against school choice: Politics, markets and fools.* Armonk, NY: M. E. Sharpe.

Smith, S. (1996). Voluntary segregation: Gender and race as legitimate grounds for differential treatment and freedom of association. In F. Margolis (Ed.), *Philosophy of Education Society 1996 yearbook.* Champaign, IL: Philosophy of Education Society.

Smith, S. S. (2004). *Boom for whom? Education, desegregation, and development in Charlotte.* Albany: State University of New York Press.

Smrekar, C., & Goldring, E. (1999). *School choice in urban America: Magnet schools and the pursuit of equity.* New York: Teachers College Press.

Sonstelie, J. (1979). Public school quality and private school enrollments. *National Tax Journal, 32*, (Supplement), 343–353.

Sonstelie, J. (1982). The welfare cost of free public schools. *Journal of Political Economy, 90*(4), 794–808.

SRI International. (1997). *Evaluation of charter school effectiveness* (Report prepared for the state of California Office of Legislative Analyst). Menlo Park, CA: Author.

St. Louis Public Schools, Division of Evaluation and Research. (1990a, November). *Post-graduation activities of 1989 high school graduates.* (A follow-up study). St. Louis: Author.

Stone, D. (2002). *Policy paradox: The art of political decision making.* New York: W. W. Norton.

Streitmatter, J. L. (1999). *For girls only: Making a case for single sex schooling.* Albany: State University of New York Press.

Sugarman, S. D., & Kemerer, F. R. (Eds.). (1999). *School choice and social controversy.* Washington, DC: Brookings Institution.

Sullivan, D., & Crain, R. L. (2000, April). *Showing that teachers matter: School segregation, staff turnover and Black student achievement.* Presentation at the annual meeting of the American Educational Research Association, New Orleans.

Swann v. Charlotte-Mecklenburg, 402 U.S. 1,15 (1971).

Taeuber, K., & James, D. (1982, April/July). Racial segregation among public and private schools. *Sociology of Education, 55*, 133–143.

Tan, N. (1990). *The Cambridge controlled choice program: Improving educational equity and integration.* New York: The Manhattan Institute, Center for Educational Innovation.

Taylor, D. G., & Alves, M. J. (1999, April). Controlled choice; Rockford, Illinois, desegregation. *Equity & Excellence in Education, 32*(1), 18–30.

Taylor, W. (2003). Title I as an instrument for achieving desegregation and equal educational opportunity. *North Carolina Law Review, 81,* 1751–1770.

*Texas Open-Enrollment Charter Schools: Third Year Evaluation.* (2000, July). Arlington: School of Urban Affairs, University of Texas at Arlington.

Tiebout, C. (1956). A pure theory of local expenditure. *Journal of Political Economy, 64,* 416–424

Trent, W. (1990). *School desegregation and successful interracial workgroups.* Unpublished paper, University of Illinois, School of Education.

Tweedie, J. (1983). The politics of legalization in special education reform. In J. Chambers & W. Hartman (Eds.), *Special education policies: Their histories, implementation, and finance* (pp. 48–112). Philadelphia: Temple University Press.

Tyack, D. (1974). *The one best system: A history of American urban education.* Cambridge, MA: Harvard University Press.

Tyack, D. (1999). Choice options: School choice—Yes, but what kind? *American Prospect Online, 10,* 6. Available at www.prospect.org/printfriendly-view. ww?id=4562

UCLA Charter School Study. (1998). *Beyond the rhetoric of charter school reform: A study of 10 California school districts.* Los Angeles: UCLA Graduate School of Education and Information Studies. Available at http:www.gseis.ucla.edu/docs/charter.pdf.

U.S. Department of Education. (2000). *The state of charter schools 2000, Fourth-year report.* Washington, DC: Author. Available at: http://www.ed.gov/pubs/charter4thyear/.

Vanourek, G., Manno, B. V., Finn, C. E., & Bierlein, L. A. (1997). *Charter schools in action project, final report: "The educational impact of charter schools."* Palo Alto, CA: Hudson Institute. Available at http://www.edexcellence.net/chart/chart5.htm.

Voluntary Interdistrct Coordinating Council (VICC). (1994, August). *Appendices to the 11th report to the United States district court, eastern district of Missouri* (Court filing G(1305)94). St. Louis, MO: Author.

Weiher, G. (1999). *Texas open-enrollment charter: Second year evaluation.* Houston: Center for Public Policy, University of Houston.

Weiher, G., Barrett, E. J., Taebel, D., Thurlow-Brenner, C., Kemmerer, F., Ausbrooks, C., et al. (1997, December). *Texas open-enrollment charter schools: Year one evaluation.* Houston: Texas State Board of Education.

Weizel, R. (1998, October 4). School busing, city and suburban. *The New York Times,* pp. 14CN, 17.

Wells, A. S. (1993). *Time to choose: America at the crossroads of school choice policy.* New York: Hill and Wang.

Wells, A. S. (2000, December). Personal communication at Study Advisory Board meeting, Berkeley, CA.

Wells, A. S. (Ed.). (2002). *Where charter school policy fails: The problems of accountability and equity.* New York: Teachers College Press.

Wells, A. S., & Crain, R. L. (1994). Perpetuation theory and the long term effects of school desegregation. *Review of Educational Research, 64*(4), 531–555.

Wells, A. S., & Crain, R. L. (1997). *Stepping over the color line: Black students in White suburbs.* New Haven, CT: Yale University Press.

Wells, A. S., Holme, J. J., Lopez, A., & Cooper, C. W. (2000). Charter schools and racial and social class segregation: Yet another sorting machine? In R. D. Kahlenberg (Ed.), *A notion at risk: Preserving public education as an engine for social mobility* (p. 356). New York: The Century Foundation Press.

Wells, A. S., Lopez, A., Scott, J., & Jellison-Holme, J. J. (1999). Charter schools as postmodern paradox: Rethinking social stratification in an age of deregulated school choice. Harvard Educational Review, 69(2), 172–204.

Wells, A. S., & Serna, I. (1996). The politics of culture: Understanding local political resistance to detracking in racially mixed schools. *Working Together Toward Reform: Harvard Educational Review, 66*(1), 28–53.

Welner, K. G. (2001). *Legal rights, local wrongs: When community control collides with educational equity.* Albany: State University of New York Press.

Whitty, G. (1997). Creating quasi-markets in education: A review of recent research on parental choice and school autonomy in three countries. In M. Apple (Ed.), *Review of Research in Education* (Vol. 22, pp. 3–47). Washington, DC: American Education Research Association.

Willie, C. V., & Alves, M. (1996). *Controlled choice: A new approach to desegregated education and school improvement* (A publication of the Education Alliance Press and the New England Desegregation Assistance Center). Providence, RI: Brown University.

Willie, C. V., Alves, M., & Hagerty, G. (1996, September). Multiracial, attractive city schools: Controlled choice in Boston. *Equity & Excellence in Education, 29*(2), 5–19.

Willie, C. V., Edwards, R., & Alves, M. J. (2002). *Student diversity, choice, and school improvement.* Westport, CT: Bergin and Garvey.

Wilms, D., & Echols, F. (1993). The Scottish experience of parental school choice. In E. Rasell & R. Rothstein (Eds.), *School choice: Examining the evidence* (pp. 63–65). Washington, DC: Economic Policy Institute.

Winerip, M. (2003). What some much-noted data really showed about vouchers. New York Times on the web. Retrieved May 7, 2003 from www.nytimes. com/2003/05/07/education/07EDUC.html?pagewanted=print&position=.

Witte, J. (1996). School choice and student performance. In H. Ladd (Ed.), *Holding schools accountable: Performance-based reform in education* (pp. 149–176). Washington, DC: Brookings Institution.

Witte, J. (2000). *The market approach to education.* Princeton, NJ: Princeton University Press.

Yancey, W. L., & Saporito, S. J. (1995). Racial and economic segregation and educational outcomes: One tale—two cities. *Applied Behavioral Science Review, 3*(2), 105–125.

Yates, L. (1997). Gender equity and the boys debate: What sort of challenge is it? *British Journal of Sociology of Education, 18*(3), 337–347.

Yudof, M. G., Kirp, D. L., & Levin, B. (1992). *Educational policy and the law* (3rd ed.). St. Paul, MN: West.

Zollers, N. (2000, March 1). Schools need rules when it comes to students with disabilities. *Education Week, 19*(25), 46.

Zollers, N. J., & Ramathan, A. K. (1998, December). For-profit charter schools and students with disabilities. *Phi Delta Kappan, 80*(4), 297–304.

Zweigenhaft, R., & Domhoff, G. (1991). *Blacks in the white establishment: A study of race and class in America.* New Haven, CT: Yale University Press.

# About the Editor
# and the Contributors

**Carol Ascher** is Senior Research Scientist at the Institute for Education and Social Policy. Her research interests focus on issues of deregulation and privatization. She has directed a national study of the opportunity to learn in charter schools in four states, as well as a 4-year study of charter school reform in New York State. The latter has appeared in several reports, most recently, *Private Partners and the Evolution of Learning Communities in Charter Schools* (2004).

**Robert L. Crain** is Professor Emeritus of Sociology and Education at Teachers College, Columbia University. He is an expert on school desegregation and is co-author (with Amy Stuart Wells) of *Stepping over the Color Line: African-American Students in White Suburban Schools* (1997).

**Amanda Datnow** is an Associate Professor at the Rossier School of Education at the University of Southern California. Her research focuses on school reform policy and politics, particularly with regard to the professional lives of educators and issues of equity.

**Jay P. Greene** is a Senior Fellow at the Manhattan Institute's Education Research Office, where he conducts research and writes about education policy. He is the author of *Education Myths*. He has conducted evaluations of school choice and accountability programs in Florida, Charlotte, Milwaukee, Cleveland, and San Antonio. He has also recently published research on high school graduation rates, charter schools, and special education. His articles have appeared in a number of policy and academic journals, as well as in major newspapers.

**Kenneth R. Howe** is Professor in the Educational Foundations, Policy, and Practice program at the University of Colorado, Boulder School of

Education, and Director of the Education and the Public Interest Center. His most recent research has focused on the school choice and education science controversies. His books include *The Ethics of Special Education* (with Ofelia Miramontes), *Understanding Equal Education: Social Justice, Democracy and Schooling, Values in Evaluation and Social Research* (with Ernest House), and *Closing Methodological Divides: Toward Democratic Educational Research.*

**Lea Hubbard** is Associate Professor of Education at the University of San Diego. Her work focuses on educational inequities as they exist across ethnicity, class, and gender. She is the coauthor (with Amanda Datnow) of *A Gendered Look at Educational Reform, Gender and Education* (2001).

**Hamilton (Hamp) Lankford** is Professor of Economics and Public Policy at the State University of New York at Albany. He currently is working with a research team to examine characteristics of teacher preparation programs that are effective in increasing the performance of students. Lankford's research on the economics of education has been published in a variety of economics and education journals and he served as an expert witness for the plaintiff in recently decided Campaign for Fiscal Equity lawsuit. He is on the editorial board of *Education Finance and Policy* and has been an American Statistical Association/National Science Foundation/Census Bureau Fellow.

**Henry M. Levin** is the William Heard Kilpatrick Professor of Economics and Education at Teachers College, Columbia University, where he is also the founder and Director of the National Center for the Study of Privatization in Education. Levin is the David Jacks Professor Emeritus of Higher Education and Economics at Stanford University. He has published over 300 articles on the economics of education; his most recent book is *Cost-Effectiveness for Education Policy* (co-authored with Patrick McEwan, 2002)

**Roslyn Arlin Mickelson** is Professor of Sociology at the University of North Carolina at Charlotte. Her research focuses upon the political economy of schooling and school reform, particularly the relationships among race, ethnicity, gender, class, and educational processes and outcomes. With support from the National Science Foundation and the Ford Foundation, she is currently investigating the consequences of unitary status on the Charlottte-Mecklenburg Schools, specifically how resegregation is influencing educational equity and academic achievement for all students. She is the author of *Children on the Streets of the Americas: Globalization, Homelessness, and Education in the United States, Brazil, and Cuba.*

**Sean F. Reardon** is Associate Professor of Education at Stanford University. His research interests include the causes and consequences of racial and socioeconomic school and residential segregation, the causes of racial and socioeconomic educational inequality, the effects of community and neighborhood context on adolescent development and behavior, and the dynamics of adult–adolescent relationships. He is currently a William T. Grant Foundation Faculty Scholar (2002–2007) and a National Academy of Education/Spencer Foundation Postdoctoral Fellow (2002–2004).

**Janelle T. Scott** is Assistant Professor at New York University's Steinhardt School of Education in the Department of Administration, Leadership, and Technology. Her research includes charter schools, educational privatization, and the impact of school choice reforms on high-poverty communities of color. Scott's recent research considers equity and empowerment within charter school communities partnered or contracted with educational management organizations, and recent resistance movements to school choice reforms.

**Nathalis Wamba** is Associate Director of the Worker Education program at Queens College, CUNY, New York. He is also an Adjunct Assistant Professor in the Department of Administration, Leadership and Technology at New York University and in the Department of Urban Studies at Queens College. His work has appeared in *Education and Urban Society, New Labor Forum, NABTE Review, Academic Exchange Quarterly, The Delaware Business Education Journal,* and *The Review (Journal of International Society for Business Education).* He is currently completing a manuscript on young workers and organized labor.

**Amy Stuart Wells** is Professor of Educational Sociology at Teachers College, Columbia University in the Department of Sociology and Education. Her research and writing has focused on race and educational policies. She is the editor of *Where Charter School Policy Fails: Issues of Accountability and Equity* (Teachers College Press, 2002); co-author (with Robert L. Crain) of *Stepping over the Color Line: African-American Students in White Suburban Schools* (1997); and author of *Time to Choose: America at the Crossroads of School Choice Policy* (1993).

**Kevin G. Welner** is Assistant Professor at the University of Colorado, Boulder School of Education, specializing in educational policy, law, and program evaluation. He is co-director of the CU-Boulder Education in the Public Interest Center (EPIC). A former attorney, he studies the intersection between education rights litigation and educational opportunity scholarship, and he is the author of *Legal Rights, Local Wrongs: When Community Control Collides with Educational Equity* (2001).

**Elisabeth (Betsey) Woody** is a Principal Research Scientist at Policy Analysis for California Education (PACE), where she directs the Public School Accountability and Effective Schools Projects. Her current research includes a mixed-method study of effective practices in low-income elementary schools and case studies of districts working to close gaps in student achievement. She recently completed a study of educators' responses to state and federal systems of accountability and how teachers and principals may use such systems to address issues of equity for students.

**James Wyckoff** is Professor of Public Administration, Public Policy and Economics, Rockefeller College of Public Affairs and Policy at State University of New York at Albany. Currently he is working with a research team to examine characteristics of teacher preparation programs that are effective in increasing the performance of students. Wyckoff is on the editorial boards of *Economics of Education Review* and *Education Finance and Policy*. He has been president of the American Education Finance Association, and a member of the board of the Education Finance Research Consortium.

**John T. Yun** is Assistant Professor at the Gevirtz Graduate School of Education, University of California, Santa Barbara. A graduate of Harvard University, Yun's research focuses on issues of equity in education, specifically patterns of school segregation; educational differences between private and public schools; the effect of funding, poverty, and opportunity on educational outcomes; and the educative/counter-educative impacts of high-stakes testing.

# Index